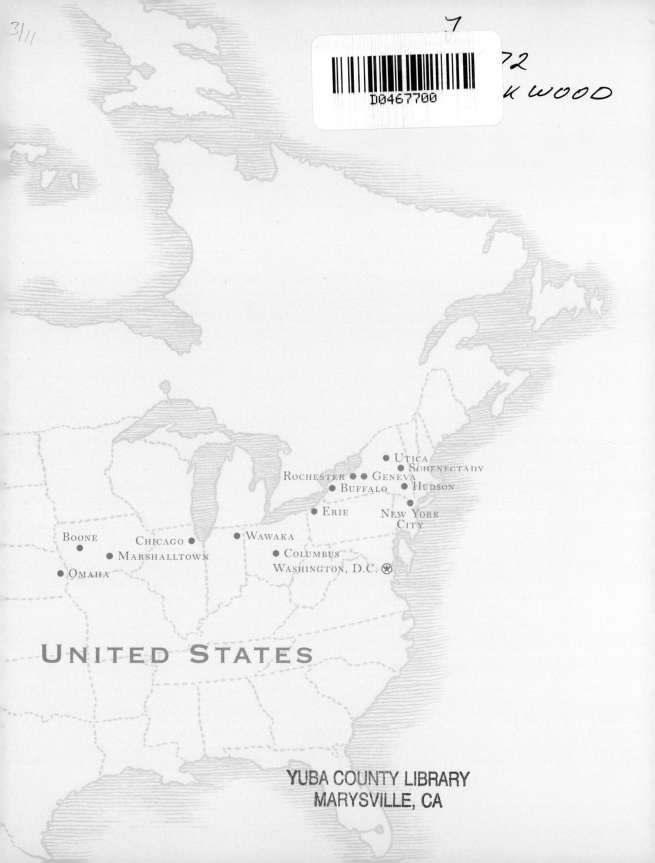

3/11

7

72

kwood

D0467700

● UTICA
● SCHENECTADY
ROCHESTER ● ● GENEVA
● BUFFALO   ● HUDSON

● ERIE   NEW YORK
                  CITY

BOONE   CHICAGO ●   ● WAWAKA
    ● MARSHALLTOWN
● OMAHA   ● COLUMBUS
              WASHINGTON, D.C. ✪

UNITED STATES

The GREAT RACE

The Amazing Round-the-World Auto Race of 1908

The GREAT RACE

The Amazing Round-the-World Auto Race of 1908

GARY BLACKWOOD

ABRAMS BOOKS FOR YOUNG READERS
NEW YORK

For Annette & Chuck

The publisher would like to thank Arnold Greenberg of the Complete Traveller Antiquarian Bookstore
in New York City.

Front endpapers: A map of many of the cities and towns the automobiles passed through on the North American leg of the race.
Title page: The cars lined up at the start.
Pages 10–11: The proposed route of the race, as depicted in the New York Times.
Pages 12–13: The De Dion with race commissioner St. Chaffray at the wheel and Captain Hansen perched behind him.
Back endpapers: A map of some of the cities and towns along the route through Asia and Europe.

Library of Congress Cataloging-in-Publication Data:

Blackwood, Gary L.
The Great Race : the amazing round-the-world auto race of 1908 / by Gary Blackwood.
p. cm.
ISBN-13: 978-0-8109-9489-8 (hardcover)
ISBN-10: 0-8109-9489-5 (hardcover)
1. Great Race (1908)—Juvenile literature. 2. Automobile racing—History—20th century—Juvenile literature.
3. Voyages around the world—History—20th century—Juvenile literature. I. Title.

GV1029.15.B54 2008
796.72—dc22
2007022414

The photographs on the front cover (except top right corner), the front jacket flap,
the bottom left corner of the back cover, the title page, and pages 16, 19, 20, 27, 29 (top),
31, 41 (top), 51, 63, and 123 courtesy of the Library of Congress.
The map on pages 10–11 and the photographs on pages 33 and 39 courtesy of the *New York Times*.
All other photographs courtesy of Frame 30 Productions.

Map illustration copyright © Bret Bertholf
Book design by Maria T. Middleton

Published in 2008 by Abrams Books for Young Readers, an imprint of Harry N. Abrams, Inc.

Printed and bound in U.S.A.
10 9 8 7 6 5 4 3 2 1

HNA
harry n. abrams, inc.
a subsidiary of La Martinière Groupe
115 West 18th Street
New York, NY 10011
www.hnabooks.com

Acknowledgments

Gathering the research materials for *The Great Race* was a painstaking process, spread out over a period of ten years or so, and I used the services of a number of different libraries. The public library of Carthage, Missouri, deserves special mention for its efforts in obtaining obscure volumes for me on interlibrary loan. So does Missouri Southern State University's Spiva Library, where I copied countless pages from its microfilm collection.

Thanks also to the National Automobile Museum in Reno for providing nuts-and-bolts information on the workings of the Thomas Flyer, to George Schuster's great-grandson Jeff Mahl for his insights, to my friends Joan Baxter and Karlheinz Eyrich for expertly translating many passages from Hans Koeppen's *Abenteuerliche Weltfahrt*, and to Antonio Scarfoglio for writing such a lively and quotable account of the race.

The author and the publisher are grateful to Michael Hamm, Jane Bisbee, and Duncan Turner of Frame 30 Productions, who generously allowed us to use hard-to-find photos from the huge stock of images they accumulated for their documentary film, *The Greatest Auto Race on Earth.*

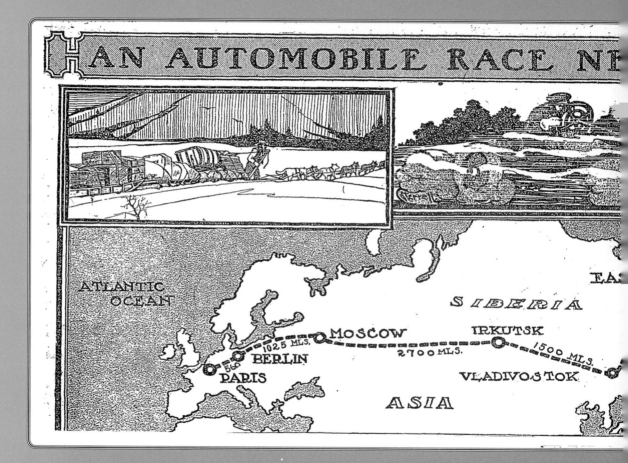

ATLANTIC
OCEAN

SIBERIA

EA

MOSCOW
IRKUTSK

1025 MLS.
2700 MLS.
1500 MLS.

BERLIN
560

PARIS
VLADIVOSTOK

ASIA

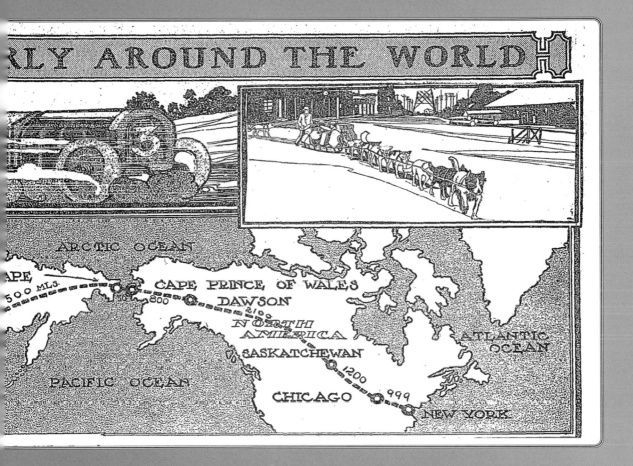

ARCTIC OCEAN

APE

500 MLS.

CAPE PRINCE OF WALES

800   DAWSON

2100

NORTH
AMERICA

SASKATCHEWAN

ATLANTIC
OCEAN

PACIFIC OCEAN

1200

CHICAGO   999

NEW YORK

MacAdam and Miller in front of the Thomas Flyer at Camp Hard Luck on the border of Manchuria.

JUNE 1, 1908

THE BORDER OF MANCHURIA,
FIFTEEN MILES WEST OF POGRANICHNAYA, SIBERIA

George MacAdam, correspondent for the *New York Times*, sat with a rifle across his knees, staring into the dark that lay beyond the small circle of light cast by the campfire. There were bandits out there somewhere on the treeless plain, ruthless Manchurian outlaws known as "red beards" who hoped to capture a rich foreign motorist or two and hold them for ransom. There were tigers, too; back in Pogranichnaya he had seen the skin of a massive beast that was shot the week before, only fifty miles away. And he had heard the unnerving sound of wolves howling in the nearby mountains.

The reporter drew out his notebook and added a few lines to the dispatch he would telegraph to the *Times*—assuming he got out of this alive. "The night was melancholy," he wrote, "and the only noise was the frog chorus. Songs failed to relieve the loneliness."

MacAdam shivered in the cold night air and wished yet again that they hadn't shipped so much of their equipment, including warm clothing, ahead by railroad. But at the time they had been only sixty miles behind the Germans. George Schuster, the driver of the American car, was sure that if they lightened their load they could put on enough extra speed to take the lead and keep it, all the way to the finish line in Paris.

There was little hope now of ever catching the Germans. The Thomas Flyer would be lucky to make it to Paris at all, let alone get there first. When the cars were crossing the United States, the Flyer had seemed indestructible, unbeatable. Now, less than two hundred miles into the Asian leg of the journey, it sat slumped on its sagging springs with a six-inch crack in its transmission case and six teeth broken off its driving gear. Next to it was a leaky makeshift tent made from scraps of canvas and rubber raincoats draped over a frame of old railroad ties. Camp Hard Luck, they had dubbed it.

Over the croaking of frogs and the murmured conversation of his companions, MacAdam heard another, more alarming sound—the crunch of footsteps approaching along the railroad tracks. He raised his rifle, cocked it, and waited, his heart in his throat, for the intruders to show themselves.

THE PLAN

The series of events that brought the Thomas Flyer and its crew to the desolate plains of Manchuria had begun six months earlier. In November 1907, the *New York Times* and the Paris newspaper *Le Matin* announced that they would cosponsor a long-distance international automobile race.

It was an audacious idea. The automobile hadn't been around for very long, and most people were not accustomed to speaking of cars and long distances

A typical street scene in 1908. Automobiles share the road with horse-drawn carriages and streetcars in Wilmington, Delaware.

in the same breath. Inventors had been devising "horseless carriages" powered by steam for almost a century, but most of them were too huge and heavy to be practical. Then, in 1890, the internal combustion gasoline engine appeared on the scene. Because it was far more compact than the typical steam engine, it could be used to power a relatively small, lightweight vehicle.

Within two years, gasoline-powered automobiles were being offered for sale to the general public. The ordinary person still considered them a novelty, a toy for the wealthy, not a reliable, proven method of transportation like the horse or the steamship or the railroad locomotive. The car manufacturers of

Europe thought otherwise. Convinced that the automobile would soon rule the transportation world, they were engaged in a fierce struggle to dominate the market. The best way for a manufacturer to prove that his machine was superior was to test it against other models on the open road. These early competitions didn't focus on speed; they were more in the nature of endurance contests.

The first auto race worthy of the name was a 130-kilometer (78-mile) dash from Paris to Rouen in 1894. It drew an astounding 102 entries. A steam-powered car built by De Dion-Bouton of France was the first to finish. The following year, America got into the act, with a race from Chicago to Evanston, Illinois. The winner averaged 7.5 miles per hour, about the speed of a leisurely bicycle ride.

The enthusiasm for these open-road contests was checked when car crashes in the 1903 Paris-to-Madrid contest took the lives of five crew members and spectators. It became known as "the Race of Death," and afterward racing in France was confined to closed tracks, to the frustration of some. "The supreme use of the automobile," complained a 1907 article in *Le Matin*, "is that it makes long journeys possible. . . . But all we have done is make it go round in circles."

The French newspaper suggested a far more ambitious race, one that would truly test the limits of men and machines: "Is there anyone who will undertake to travel this summer from Paris to Peking by automobile?" Within a week, ten carmakers and drivers from various European countries had accepted the challenge. The Marquis de Dion, whose auto had won the Paris–Rouen contest, called *Le Matin*'s proposal "a real Jules Verne undertaking," referring to the author of the popular adventure novel *Around the World in Eighty Days*.

As it turned out, the race went in the other direction—from Peking to Paris. *Le Matin* insisted on calling it a *raid*, or endurance test; the important thing, the paper pointed out, was not which car finished first, but how well the machines held up over a grueling course that covered roughly ten thousand miles. As *Autocar* magazine put it, "All competitors finishing within a reasonable time will be considered to have accomplished a performance of equal merit." But the French were confident that their cars would be first among equals.

By the time the race began on June 10, 1907, only five entries remained. The French accounted for three of them—two De Dions and a tiny, three-wheeled Tri-Contal, a sort of overgrown motorcycle. There was also an auto from Italy and one from the Netherlands. Only a day or two out of Peking, the drivers' natural competitive spirit kicked in, and the *raid* turned into a speed contest. After two months of bone-jarring and frame-rattling travel over pitiful roads or, more often, no roads at all, the first auto reached Paris. It was not, as expected, one of the De Dions, but the Italian car. Nearly three more weeks passed before the remaining autos turned up—or rather, three of them did. The little Tri-Contal had run out of gas in the middle of the Gobi Desert. The French cars' poor showing was a considerable embarrassment for the Marquis de Dion, and for French automakers in general, who for decades had considered themselves the leaders of the industry.

A mere nine weeks after the De Dions came limping home, the marquis was given a chance to redeem himself.

Le Matin had seen the Peking–Paris contest partly as a way of promoting the French auto industry. That hadn't worked out so well. But the newspaper had another, more selfish, motive—boosting its circulation—and that had worked out wonderfully; the public couldn't seem to get enough of the drivers' harrowing, sometimes life-threatening exploits.

And who could blame them? The period around the turn of the twentieth century was an unstable, unsettling time. The world was tormented by wars and rumors of wars: In 1894, China fought Japan for control of Korea in the Sino-Japanese War. In 1898, the destruction of the battleship *Maine* ignited the Spanish-American War. The following year, Britain began battling the Boers, Dutch settlers in South Africa. In 1904, Korea, along with Manchuria, became a battleground again; this time the combatants were Russia and Japan.

There was no shortage of revolts and rebellions, either. Two of the most significant were the Boxer Rebellion (1898–1900), an attempt by the Chinese to drive foreign powers out of their country, and a 1905 peasant revolt in Russia, which forced Tsar Nicholas II to make some major reforms.

The mast of the sunken USS Maine *is visible above the waters of Cuba. An explosion in the fore of the ship, believed to be caused by an underwater mine planted by the Spanish, killed 266 sailors and helped lead to the Spanish-American War over Cuban independence.*

Even countries that weren't actually at war were preparing for the possibility. Germany and France had squared off back in 1870–71, in the Franco-Prussian War, and each still felt so threatened by the other that they made deals with other countries for mutual defense. The Germans joined forces with Italy and with the crumbling Austro-Hungarian Empire; France allied itself with Britain and Russia.

No wonder the public was so eager to read about a more benign sort of rivalry, one that involved automobiles, not armies. The newspapers were glad to oblige. And if a race halfway around the world attracted readers, what better way to keep them than by sponsoring another, even more ambitious contest, one that spanned the entire globe—minus the oceans, of course. On November 24, 1907, *Le Matin* announced a New York–to–Paris race.

Jules Verne's fictional account of a globe-circling journey, *Around the World in Eighty Days*, had created a sensation when it was published in 1873 and inspired a series of real-life attempts to surpass Phileas Fogg's imaginary feat.

Several intrepid travelers succeeded, including Elizabeth Cochrane, a twenty-five-year-old reporter for the *New York World*. Cochrane, who set off in 1889, made the trip in seventy-two days. Her lively accounts of her adventures, written under the byline Nellie Bly, helped turn the *World* into one of the city's most popular papers.

In 1892, George Train beat her record by twelve days. Like Cochrane, Train relied, appropriately enough, on trains and ships for transportation. Though autos came on the market that same year, no one was foolish enough to try taking one around the world until 1902, when Dr. E. C. Lehwess of London set out in a three-ton enclosed

Intrepid journalist Nellie Bly (née Elizabeth Cochrane) traveled around the world in a then record-breaking seventy-two days via ship, train, wagon, carriage, and rickshaw.

truck—an early version of a motor home—which he christened Passepartout, after Phileas Fogg's faithful sidekick.

Lehwess made the trip into a sort of extended holiday, laying over for weeks at a time in Paris and Berlin, Warsaw and St. Petersburg. After nine months, he tired of the whole thing and returned to London. His crew kept going, but not for long. About 250 miles east of Moscow, the Russian cold cracked the engine block, ending the Passepartout's oddball odyssey.

Over the next several years, other drivers, undaunted by Lehwess's failure, undertook a series of seemingly impossible journeys, determined to prove the auto industry's claim that "As long as a man has a car he can do anything and go anywhere." By the end of 1907, automobiles had crossed the United States, Europe, and Asia. (Within two years, they would conquer Australia and Africa as well.) Ernest Shackleton, the Antarctic explorer, was even talking of a drive to the South Pole. But no one had yet managed to take on three continents at a single go.

Just working out the logistics of such a trip was a staggering task. For one thing, it required countries with a history of making war on one another to actually cooperate instead. To head up the race committee, *Le Matin* chose Georges Bourcier St. Chaffray, who had helped organize the Peking–Paris contest. The fact that he was the Marquis de Dion's nephew may also have worked in his favor.

Not content with just being in charge of the race, St. Chaffray claimed that the whole thing was his idea. This raised a howl of protest from Eugene Lelouvier, a boastful adventurer who had laid out part of the Peking-to-Paris route by crossing the Gobi Desert on foot disguised as a Chinese man. Lelouvier insisted that *he* had been the first to propose a round-the-world race.

After the *New York Times* signed on as cosponsor, it was agreed that the race would begin in Times Square in New York City. The most practical strategy would have been to cross the United States in late summer, when the existing roads—nearly all of them unpaved—were dry and solid. The vehicles could then be shipped to Siberia, where they could follow the 5,400-mile network of wagon trails known as the great Russian post road; with any luck, the road, a morass of mud in warm weather, would be frozen solid by then.

But St. Chaffray was not a practical man. Instead of consulting someone who actually knew firsthand the territory that the race would cross, he preferred to rely on maps to lay out the course. On a map it looked entirely possible to make the whole trip by land. According to St. Chaffray's plan, the autos would drive to San Francisco or Seattle, head north along the coast of British Columbia to Alaska, use the frozen Yukon River as a road to the coast, then cross the Bering Stait on the ice. They could drive along the Lena River through northern Siberia to Irkutsk; from there, like the Peking–Paris racers, they would follow the Trans-Siberian Railway to Europe. Of course, in order to make sure the rivers and the Bering Strait were frozen, the cars would have to start out in the dead of winter. Though the famed Arctic explorer Roald Amundsen felt that the route might be feasible, most experts declared it "impractical and foolhardy." According to another explorer, Harry de Windt, who had nearly died crossing the Bering Strait by sled six years earlier, "A preliminary survey would speedily demonstrate the utter absurdity of the New York–Paris expedition." The strait, he pointed out, was seldom frozen completely, and even when it was, the ice was not smooth and level, but a jagged landscape of peaks and crevasses.

Not surprisingly, Eugene Lelouvier—still outraged at getting no credit for the race—found St. Chaffray's plans totally unsuitable. He announced that he would drive to Paris independently of the other entries, using a far superior route, and convinced the *New York World*, the paper that had sent Nellie Bly around the world, to finance him.

Others found the notion of crossing the Arctic wasteland in an automobile downright laughable. Before the race even began, one wit composed a series of telegrams supposedly wired from Alaska by the contestants. "Busy trying to make gasoline out of whale oil," read one fake message. "Tried it yesterday. Result, machine immediately spouted and dived through hole in ice. Chauffeur had to harpoon it to get it ashore." Another reported that a driver had been arrested for "exceeding the upper Alaskan speed limit of one mile in 60 hours."

Lelouvier at the wheel of the Werner, his unofficial entry in the New York–Paris race. His driver sits beside him.

It wasn't just the daunting terrain, though, that made the journey seem impossible. It was also the notoriously unreliable nature of the automobile—which, after all, had been around for less than two decades. "It must be borne in mind," wrote a reporter for the London *Daily Mail*, "that the motor car, after woman, is the most fragile and capricious thing on earth." But for every skeptic who dismissed the automobile as "an ingenious toy," there was a hard-core enthusiast who insisted that "the motor-car is the machine of the future, and nothing can stop its progress." Ironically, the man who said this was Auguste Pons, whose tiny Tri-Contal, his entry in the Peking–Paris race, sat abandoned in the Gobi Desert.

THE CARS

On January 18, the *Times* reported that ten cars had signed on for the New York–to–Paris race. The French, determined to win this time, had three entries. There were two Italian cars, one German, and four American. It soon became obvious that not all of these "entries" were legitimate contenders. Several manufacturers had entered merely as a way of getting free publicity and had no intention of actually starting. By the eve of the race, the field had narrowed to six, plus one unofficial entry—a vehicle built by the Werner company and driven by that egotistical maverick Lelouvier.

The route had undergone some changes, too. To make sure they reached Alaska before the snow and ice began to thaw, when the cars reached San Francisco, they would be shipped to Seattle, then to Valdez, Alaska. The race committee had finally realized, too, how risky driving across the Bering Strait would be. The cars would make the trip from Nome, Alaska, to Siberia aboard another ship.

Of course, once the snow and ice began to melt, it would be impossible to drive across Alaska. The race committee discussed shipping the cars by rail across part of the United States, to make sure they got to Valdez before the spring thaw. This was not officially part of the plan, only a possibility, but apparently some of the contestants thought it was a given. The misunderstanding would cause major problems later on.

Even with these improvements in the route, none but the most blindly optimistic of automobile advocates expected all or even most of the cars to actually reach Paris. Novelist Rex Beach, who had lived in Alaska, bet a friend a thousand dollars that none of the machines would make it. Apparently the sponsors had their doubts, too. The *Times* announced that the winner would be not necessarily the first one to Paris, but "that automobile which . . . shall reach the point in the itinerary which is farthest from the starting point."

The cars generally considered to be the top contenders were the French entries—or, rather, two of the French entries. Hardly anyone except the manufacturer and the driver held out much hope for the third, a little Sizaire-Naudin with a fifteen-horsepower "one-lunger" (one-cylinder engine); all the other entries had four cylinders, and so were much more powerful. The *Times* called it "the most remarkable vehicle entered in the race"—a polite way of saying that it was hopelessly undersized and underpowered.

The other competitors regarded the Sizaire-Naudin with amusement. "Because of its size and delicacy," wrote the head of the German team, "we have to try not to laugh. . . . Behind the driver's seat is just a suitcase, with the supplies for the journey. They probably even have their fuel supply in that suitcase."

THE OFFICIAL ENTRIES

CAR	COUNTRY	WEIGHT	CYLINDERS*	HORSEPOWER	DRIVE**
Sizaire-Naudin	France	3,300 lbs.	1	15	Shaft
Moto-Bloc	France	6,400 lbs.	4	30	Chain
De Dion	France	6,600 lbs.	4	30	Shaft
Protos	Germany	8,000 lbs.	4	40	Shaft
Zust	Italy	3,500 lbs.	4	30	Chain
Thomas	United States	5,700 lbs.	4	60	Chain

*The cylinders are where the gasoline, mixed with air, is ignited by the spark plugs, providing the power to run the car; the more cylinders a vehicle has, and the larger they are, the more powerful it is.

The drive train usually consists of three elements: 1) The **transmission, a set of gears that transmits power from the engine to the drive shaft; the gears can be shifted to different "speeds." 2) A **driveshaft** that delivers the power to the differential at the rear of the car; half the 1908 entries used chains and sprockets instead, much like those on a bicycle. 3) The **differential**, a gearbox that transfers the power to the wheels.

The Moto-Bloc, the second French entry, was literally twice the size of the Sizaire Naudin, with double the horsepower. According to its crew, the car was "solid as a battering ram." From behind, it more nearly resembled a chuck wagon. A huge chest of drawers built into the back contained an impressive array of cold-weather gear, spare parts, and supplies, including several bottles of champagne for celebrating the anticipated victory.

Like all the cars, the Moto-Bloc was designed for durability, not comfort. It had no windshield in the modern sense, just a leather screen that came up to the driver's chin. There was no real roof, either, only a convertible-style top that could be fitted into place over the cab.

The third French car, almost identical to the Moto-Bloc in size and horsepower, was made by De Dion-Bouton, the company that had fared so poorly in the Peking–Paris contest. The *Times* considered the De Dion "the best prepared of any of the machines entering in the race." The drivers from the Peking–Paris race had helped design this new model. In addition, "many of the devices included in its unique equipment were added upon the suggestion of Hans Hendrik Hansen, the Arctic explorer, who will accompany the car."

The "unique equipment" included curtains that hung to the ground to protect the crew from nasty weather; a hand-cranked generator that ran an electric light; a chassis (frame) lined with soft wood and wrapped with cloth to protect the steel from cracking in the intense cold; seven gas tanks that held a total of 700 liters (185 gallons), which was twice as much as the Moto-Bloc held and about eight times the fuel capacity of a modern SUV; and a mast that Hansen intended to fit out with a sail so that, in the unlikely event that they ever ran out of gas, they could propel the car by wind power. (Actually, 185 gallons of gas wouldn't last as long as you might expect; the cars typically got seven or eight miles per gallon—roughly the same as today's large motor homes.)

The German Protos Company entered the race only a month before it began. Its car was built like a tank (though actual tanks wouldn't be in use for another six years) and was accordingly heavy—8,000 pounds, compared to about 6,500 for the Moto-Bloc and De Dion. It was equipped with a forty-horsepower engine—

LEFT: *The little Sizaire-Naudin, with the De Dion to its left, lines up at the start of the New York–Paris race in Times Square, New York City.*

BELOW: *The second French entry, the Moto-Bloc, with Godard at the wheel, just before the start of the race.*

larger than the French cars had, but still pretty small for all that weight. By comparison, a typical modern SUV, which weighs about the same, has at least three hundred horsepower. The Protos boasted no fewer than six gas tanks, connected by yards of copper pipe that snaked across the floor of the vehicle. Like the others, it had a detachable canvas top; with the top in place, it resembled a covered wagon.

The Germans carried even more equipment than the French crews. Their list of supplies was literally three feet long. An American sportsman who examined the car before the race commented, "There you can see German efficiency. . . . There's nothing missing, not an axe or saw, tent or sleeping bag—things the others didn't even think of. And how neatly everything is packed away. I think the German boys will make it."

Two Italian automakers had announced that they would enter the race, but Itala, the company whose auto won the Peking–Paris contest, withdrew when its driver fell ill. The other entry came from the Zust Company. Its engineers had started with their smallest stock chassis, added a custom-built light body, then equipped it with a large engine and a transmission with lower gears than normal, for extra traction. The resulting machine weighed only two hundred pounds more than the little Sizaire-Naudin but had as much power as the Moto-Bloc and the De Dion.

The American entry, the Thomas Flyer, was the wild card in the pack. Though companies in the United States had been turning out cars for more than ten years, their reputations and their sales figures couldn't match those of European makers. And the E. R. Thomas Motor Company wasn't even a major player in the American auto industry. Very few buyers could afford the Flyer's hefty four-thousand-dollar price tag—the equivalent of ninety thousand in today's dollars. In 1907, the company had sold only seven hundred of its standard models, compared with the five thousand or more turned out by such makers as Cadillac and Packard.

The Flyer was another last-minute entry. When Thomas dealers in New York and Chicago had first tried to convince the company's founder, E. R. Thomas, that

LEFT: *The third French entry, the De Dion-Bouton, at the start. The crew wear special cold-weather gear.*

BELOW: *The German entry, the tanklike Protos, at the start.*

the race would be good publicity, Thomas, a conservative man who disliked taking risks, had said no. "None of those cars will reach Chicago," he told his employees.

Something, or someone, changed his mind. By the end of January, Thomas had done a complete about-face: "It would be a disgrace . . . if our country was not represented in the race, which is the greatest event that has ever happened in the history of the automobile industry or any other sport."

By this time, it was too late to design and build a special machine for the race. The company's engineers chose a stock 1907 Flyer originally destined for a customer in Boston. They made only a few alterations, including bolting a searchlight to the hood and adding a detachable canvas top like those on the French and German cars. According to the *Times*, there were also a number of holes drilled through the floorboards, so the heat from the engine would warm the driver's feet.

The Flyer was built for speed. At 5,700 pounds, it was almost as heavy as the De Dion and Moto-Bloc, but its huge 571-cubic-inch engine produced sixty horsepower—twice that of the French cars. It was also designed for hill climbing, a popular sport at the time. To keep the Flyer from rolling backward on steep slopes, it was equipped with the "Thomas Back Stop Safety Device," a ratchet mechanism that, when engaged, let the wheels turn in only one direction: forward.

It's doubtful that E. R. Thomas seriously expected his car to win. He told the *Times* he was "confident not only that the car will make a most creditable showing in the trip across the continent, but that it will go as far in the entire race as any of the foreign machines." But the Thomas didn't carry nearly as extensive a supply of food, cold-weather gear, and spare parts as the other entries.

The French De Dion crew went so far as to declare, "We do not consider the Thomas car in the New York and Paris race. . . . We have known all along that they were not equipped for the Alaskan trip or the Siberian journey." They accused the company of entering, like those early dropouts, only for "advertising purposes."

SCARFOGLIO IN N.Y.-PARIS RACE 2/12/08
22-10

LEFT: *The Italian entry, the Zust, decorated with flags before the race. Many of the race fans gathered in Times Square were Italian immigrants who were cheering for the Zust to win.*

BELOW: *The late entry, the American Thomas Flyer, with Monty Roberts at the wheel. Many thought the American car had entered as a publicity stunt and had little chance of finishing the race.*

N.Y. PARIS RACE - ROBERTS IN THOMAS CAR
22-9

They were overlooking the fact that the Thomas crew hadn't had much time to prepare—and the fact that, unlike the foreign entrants, the Americans could have supplies and parts shipped to them easily and quickly by rail during the U.S. leg of the race.

In any case, as the *Times* pointed out, how much stuff a team carried wasn't the most important factor. "It will be the personal pluck and ingenuity of the driver that will bring victory to a car rather than the equipment. . . . It is the man and not the machine that will win the New York to Paris race."

THE MEN

There was plenty of pluck and ingenuity among the race crews, though they came from different backgrounds and had widely varied driving experience. Some had raced before but two didn't know how to drive at all.

The driver of the race's acknowledged underdog, the little Sizaire-Naudin, was none other than Auguste Pons, the Frenchman who eight months earlier, in the Peking–Paris race, had nearly met his end in the Gobi Desert along with his glorified motorcycle. Pons, a muscular, athletic man, was well known in racing circles for his daring and his determination—stubbornness might be a better term. Though he had a wife and family to care for (his four-year-old daughter, Lily, would grow up to be a world-famous opera singer), he couldn't resist the challenge of a round-the-world race.

He had apparently learned nothing from his near-death experience in the Peking–Paris race. He was still convinced that a small, light vehicle was more sensible than a large, heavy one because it used less gas and was not so likely to bog down on muddy roads—and if it did get stuck or break down, it would be easier to push.

OPPOSITE: *The contestants (and friends), minus the American team, from left to right: Julian Bloc, Ernest Maas, Hans Koeppen, R. Maurice Livier, Arthur Hue, Antonio Scarfoglio, Charles Godard, Hans Knape, G. Bourcier St. Chaffray, Hans Hendrik Hansen, Autran, Emilio Sitori, Henri Haaga, Auguste Pons, Maurice Berthe, W. J. Hanley, Lucien Deschamps, Fred J. Swentzel.*

Somehow he managed to cram two crewmen into the car with him; since the Sizaire-Naudin had only two seats, one of the men must have perched in back with the suitcase.

The second French entry, the Moto-Bloc, would be piloted by a fellow veteran of the Peking–Paris race, Charles Godard. Godard had a well-earned reputation as a rogue, a daredevil, and a bit of a clown. Before entering the Peking–Paris contest, he had been a motorcycle stunt rider, starring in a fairground spectacle known as the Wall of Death.

He had talked the Spyker Company of Holland into letting him drive their car in the Peking–Paris race, assuring them that he would foot the bill. He proceeded to sell the car's spare parts to pay for his steamship ticket—first class, of course—to Peking, where he conned several people into lending him money to complete the race. When Godard reached Europe, he was arrested and threatened with prison if he didn't repay his debts.

Undaunted, Godard, trading on the notoriety the race had brought him, borrowed enough money to pay off his debts, then found some wealthy investors to help him start his own car company, Moto-Bloc. Godard was no businessman; he was less interested in manufacturing automobiles than in driving them—as fast as possible. But when the New York–Paris race was announced, he realized it was the perfect opportunity to promote his product—and, at the same time, have a grand adventure.

THE CAPTAINS & THEIR CREWS

CAR	CREW NAMES	NATIONALITY	AGE
Sizaire-Naudin	**Auguste Pons**	French	32
	Maurice Berthe	French	24
	Lucien Deschamps	French	24
Moto-Bloc	**Charles Godard**	French	31
	Arthur Hue	French	26
	R. Maurice Livier	French	19
De Dion	**G. Bourcier St. Chaffray**	French	36
	Autran	French	25
	Hans Hendrik Hansen	Norwegian	43
Protos	**Hans Koeppen**	German	31
	Ernest Maas	German	33
	Hans Knape	German	29
Zust	**Antonio Scarfoglio**	Italian	21
	Emilio Sitori	Italian	26
	Henri Haaga	German	22
Thomas	**Montague Roberts**	American	25
	George Schuster	American	35

As always, he managed to raise the money for the race, which, according to an early estimate in the *Times*, would cost each entry at least ten thousand dollars. Finding a crew was even easier; there was no shortage of young men willing to share in the adventure. Godard chose cameraman Arthur Hue, who planned to sell films of the trip, and mechanic R. Maurice Livier, at nineteen the youngest of all the race's participants.

The third French car, the De Dion, had the most celebrated crew member, Hans Hendrik Hansen. The Norwegian engineer and explorer had gained fame in 1897 when he tried (unsuccessfully) to rescue an adventurer named Andrée, who was lost while trying to float his hot-air balloon over the North Pole. Hansen was the only contestant who had actually spent time in Siberia and could speak Russian. In fact, he was married to a Russian woman—a fact that did not deter him from flirting shamelessly with every attractive woman who crossed his path.

Though Hansen, at forty-three, was the oldest man in the race, he had more energy than many of the younger men and was perpetually, sometimes maddeningly, cheerful—as long as things went his way. Judging from the stories he told at every opportunity, he had been nearly everywhere and done nearly everything. He had helped put down a revolution in Argentina; he had built railroads across South America, Mexico, and the Rocky Mountains; he had prospected for gold and oil in Siberia; he had even, he claimed, sailed a Viking ship from Norway to Chicago for the 1893 World's Fair. The one thing he had never done was learn to drive. He came aboard the De Dion as the car's navigator. Though he liked to be addressed as "Captain Hansen," there's no evidence that he ever actually held that rank; more likely it was an honorary title.

Captain Hans Hendrik Hansen, a Norwegian explorer and adventurer, claimed to speak seven languages and to have lived for many years in Siberia. Though he had worked on railroads and ships, he didn't know how to drive a car.

Taking the wheel of the De Dion was the commissioner general of the race himself, G. Bourcier St. Chaffray. He was a thin man with an aristocratic air and a biting wit. He was something of a dandy; while most of the contestants sported mustaches, he was clean-shaven. He was also a bit of a braggart, as fond as Hansen of talking about himself and his exploits. And, like Hansen, he insisted on doing things his own way; the two would prove to be an explosive combination.

With practice, nearly anyone could manage to drive a car adequately if he or she was strong enough to control the stubborn steering wheel. The real challenge was fixing the machines when they broke down, as they so often did. On the De Dion, that chore fell to a young mechanic known only as Autran.

Lieutenant Hans Koeppen, captain of the German team, was an ambitious military officer, with skills as a horseman, marksman, and tennis player, but, like Hansen, knew very little about driving cars.

The three Germans who manned the massive Protos were supposed to be equal partners, but the one who received the most attention from the press was Hans Koeppen, a tall, dashing German army officer. Beneath a polite, good-humored exterior, Koeppen had a will of iron. He would need it.

Though the emperor of Germany, Kaiser Wilhelm, was an avid motorist with a stable of seventeen vehicles, the country's auto manufacturers had doubts about sending a car around the world. Winning the race would undoubtedly increase the demand for German-made autos. But what if the German entry finished last, or didn't finish at all? That wouldn't help business. Hans Koeppen was more confident. He was eager to promote German autos, and particularly to show that they were reliable enough for military use. He saw the race as the perfect chance to do both those things. Even more important, it was an opportunity to promote himself. After fourteen years of service, the thirty-one-year-old was still stuck in the rank of lieutenant. Since Germany was at peace—for the moment, anyway—he couldn't prove himself in battle. The chance to defeat other countries in an automobile race was the nearest he could get to a war.

Koeppen visited thirty car manufacturers, including Daimler and Benz, before he finally found one that would even consider entering. The director of the Protos Company reluctantly agreed to provide a car and spare parts. He even sent along two of his best engineers to keep the car running—and, as it turned out, to do the driving. Though Koeppen was a skilled horseman, tennis player, and marksman, he admitted that he knew as much about driving a car as he did about piloting a dirigible.

Unfortunately, the firm wasn't willing to put any cold cash into such a risky venture. The German newspaper *Zeitung am Mittag* contributed fifteen hundred dollars, but that barely covered the entry fee. Koeppen invested three thousand dollars of his own modest fortune. The two engineers, Hans Knape and Ernest Maas, had such confidence in their car that they kicked in an additional three thousand dollars each.

The Protos factories typically built their autos to order, a process that took five or six weeks, and even longer for a specially equipped model. But the race was scheduled to start on February 12, which gave them only thirty days from the time they agreed to enter a car to build one. Though the company was stingy with its money, it was more than generous with its manpower; it put six hundred employees to work on the project. On January 26, the car was completed. Three days later, it was on board a ship heading for America.

Koeppen felt sure that he could take the car all the way to Paris. In truth, he felt he had no choice. It was his duty to the German army and to the kaiser, who personally granted him a six-month leave of absence. The lieutenant later said—again comparing the race to a battle—that he was inspired by "the famous command which was given our troops" during the Boxer Rebellion, "'Germans to the front.'"

The Italian car, the Zust, had less trouble finding financing. The Naples newspaper *Il Mattino* agreed to sponsor it. Antonio Scarfoglio, the twenty-one-year-old son of the paper's owner, secured a seat in the car by promising to send regular dispatches by telegraph to *Il Mattino* and to the London *Daily Mail*. When his father objected, Antonio—a would-be poet with a pronounced flair for the dramatic—announced that if he couldn't enter the race, he would do something even more dangerous, such as taking a motorboat across the Atlantic Ocean.

Scarfoglio had little experience with either motorboats or cars. According to the *Times*, he was "an amateur driver, and has entered the race from a sporting spirit and a desire for adventure." Needing a more seasoned driver, the Zust Company hired Emilio Sitori, a twenty-six-year-old professional chauffeur.

Just before the car was shipped to America, a German mechanic from the Zust factory joined the crew. Henri Haaga had been in Italy only a few months and, to Scarfoglio's disgust, spoke no Italian. Though Haaga was a year older than Scarfoglio, the reporter referred to him as "this big, blond baby." Because its crew looked so young, the Zust was labeled "the children's car."

Two days before the race, the Zust developed a major problem—

Antonio Scarfoglio, captain of the Italian car, was among the youngest and wealthiest of the competitors. He was the son of the owner of the newspaper that sponsored the Italian car. He was also a poet who would write colorful accounts of the race.

a broken tube on the injector, the apparatus that fed motor oil into the cylinders. It gave Haaga a chance to prove his worth. Though he was no wizard with languages, in mechanical matters he had no equal. By the following day he had the car running perfectly.

Montague Roberts, the captain of the Thomas Flyer, was not quite the celebrity Captain Hansen was. But in racing circles he was well known and respected. He had driven Thomas cars to victory in several major races, including a grueling twenty-four-hour endurance contest the previous year. Between races, he delivered Thomas cars to such notable customers as the young Franklin Roosevelt, the future president, who also had Roberts give him driving lessons.

Montague Roberts, captain of the American car, had made a name for himself racing in numerous auto trials and endurance contests. He was credited with charming the reluctant E. R. Thomas, owner of the Thomas Company, into entering a car in the race.

Roberts trained for each race as rigorously as a boxer getting ready for the ring, and it showed. A reporter for the *Times* declared that "a better man than Montague Roberts could hardly have been selected to drive the car. He is a young man, barely 25 years of age, of good physique, and the hard work to which he has been inured during the last few years has given him a splendid physical constitution." Monty was as eager for adventure as Scarfoglio and as confident of victory as Koeppen. His enthusiasm quickly earned him the nickname "Get There Roberts."

If the charming, outgoing Roberts was the star of the American team, its mainstay was modest, methodical George Schuster. In his younger years, Schuster had worked in his father's blacksmith shop, where he learned how to forge and weld steel. Though he was small, the work had made him surprisingly strong.

For a time, he built and raced bicycles, but then he became fascinated by automobiles. After selling cars on his own for several years, he took a job at the Thomas factory in Buffalo. Now, at the age of thirty-five, he was the company's chief troubleshooter, helping customers as far away as Puerto Rico fix whatever problems plagued their autos. He was an experienced driver, too; in 1907, he had taken five newspaper reporters on a four-state tour in a Thomas car.

Early in February, three days before the start of the race, Monty Roberts offered Schuster a seat on the Flyer, but the older man thought he was joking; after all, E. R. Thomas had said in no uncertain terms that the company wouldn't be entering a car. Schuster didn't know yet that the boss had changed his mind, probably thanks to Monty's enthusiasm. On February 11, Schuster got a call summoning him to New York City to join Roberts. Though the troubleshooter was reluctant to leave his wife and his young son for months on end, the money was too good to pass up: fifty dollars a week—double his usual salary—plus a thousand-dollar bonus if the Flyer finished first.

He had one day to prepare himself for a trip around the world.

THE RACE, FEBRUARY 11–17

The race was scheduled to start at 11:00 A.M. on February 12. Eugene Lelouvier, the renegade Frenchman who had disapproved of everything else about the contest, found that unacceptable, too. He set out a day earlier than the others, as an unofficial contestant, boasting that he would "be in Paris much more than a day ahead of them."

Lelouvier apparently subscribed to Auguste Pons's theory that smaller is better. His entry was a diminutive auto made by the Werner Company of France. It was only a little larger than the Sizaire-Naudin and had the same size engine—a paltry fifteen horsepower. A crew of two were crammed into the vehicle with him.

LEFT: *The maverick contestant Lelouvier preparing to start a day early, on February 11, 1908.*

BELOW: *Times Square, packed with race fans on the morning of February 12, 1908.*

The route mapped out so arbitrarily by Commissioner General St. Chaffray cut across the middle of New York State, skirted the shores of the Great Lakes, then made a beeline through the Midwest and the Great Plains before turning southwest across Nevada and California. Lelouvier steered a more southerly course that—theoretically, anyway—would take him through Pittsburgh, Cincinnati, and St. Louis.

The morning after Lelouvier's departure, the six *official* entries lined up in Times Square. The square was so packed with spectators—some fifty thousand of them, according to one report—that there wasn't much room for the cars. Though a ring of policemen tried to hold the crowd back, people surged forward and mobbed the motorists, eager to wish their favorites bon voyage—or *buono viaggio*, or godspeed, or *Gute Reise*, depending on the well-wisher's nationality. The United States was, after all, a land of immigrants, and for a large proportion of those following the race, it was not about the men or the machines; it was about national pride.

As the *Times* put it, "Patriotism has made America pin its faith to the pluck and skill of the drivers of the car which carries the Stars and Stripes. For a like reason France has high hopes for those that bear the tri-color, while Germany is grimly determined that her own entry shall be first at the finish, and Italy has the same buoyant faith." Many of those who had immigrated from Europe were rooting for the entry that represented their old homeland.

The fans' fervor was fueled by competing bands playing the various national anthems, and by the flags that fluttered everywhere, bearing the colors of the rival countries. Sometimes a note of paranoia or prejudice crept into the patriotic sentiments. A banner outside the Thomas dealership read, "America Against the World." One automobilist declared, "I'll back an American to win over a foreigner any time when ingenuity, endurance, and determination are at stake."

As for the crew members themselves, though most of them weren't quite as fervent as the proudly German Lieutenant Koeppen, they had their share of patriotic feelings, and they weren't immune to the long-standing grudges that existed between some of the nations of Europe. Though the Franco-Prussian War had ended in 1871, there was still a good deal of animosity between France and Germany as a result of the conflict. There was no love lost between the French and Italians, either, after Italy's triumph in the Peking–Paris race. Nor were the Italians, by and large, very fond of Germans. Despite the presence of the skilled and affable Henri Haaga on his crew, the Italian reporter Antonio Scarfoglio was prone to comments about "the terrible German race." Of course, he also generally disliked the Japanese and Chinese, not to mention Americans, whom he characterized as a materialistic people without a past.

Scarfoglio, who was at heart a poet, not a journalist, even claimed that the autos themselves possessed a sort of national character, in keeping with the country where they were made: "Each nation seems to have put a reflex of its soul into these machines . . . created in their own likeness—the Protos, heavy and strong to labour; the Thomas, long and impetuous, straining like a greyhound at the leash; the Zust, Motobloc, and Sizaire, slender and nervous."

Whether or not the cars were nervous, the drivers surely were, as 11 o'clock came and went and there was no sign of the mayor, who was to signal the beginning of the race. As it turned out, he had been misinformed about the starting time. At 11:15, the president of the Automobile Club of America took it upon himself to fire the gold-plated starter pistol.

The drivers, however, didn't put the pedal to the metal. For one thing, not all the cars had gas pedals (the Flyer's accelerator, for example, was a lever located on the steering wheel). For another, they were still hemmed in by spectators. Instead of roaring away from the finish line, wrote Scarfoglio, they crept along "between two thick hedges of extended hands" and were "kissed again and again," while the Zust's supporters cheered, "Italy! Italy! Hurrah!"

Finally, in Yonkers, twelve miles from Times Square, the crowds thinned out, the escort cars turned back, and the race began in earnest. Despite their differences, the French and the Germans agreed on one thing: There was no point in pouring on the speed this early. It would only put a strain on the cars. As Lieutenant Koeppen said, "Farness is better than fastness in so long a race."

RIGHT: *The cars line up at the start of the race, awaiting the pistol, as policemen attempt to clear the route ahead.*

BELOW: *The Italian Zust makes its way through Utica, New York, with the American Flyer coming up behind.*

Surprisingly, the Moto-Bloc's driver, the speed-crazy Charles Godard, echoed that sentiment: "Who goes slowly, goes far."

The Italians and the Americans had a different strategy: Take the lead as soon as possible and keep it. That was more easily said than done. Outside the city, the roads were covered in snow, and the farther the cars went, the deeper it got.

The Italian Zust was out in front for a time, just long enough to give Scarfoglio delusions of victory. Then the car's radiator sprang a leak. Haaga, the mechanical genius, quickly repaired it but couldn't refill it. The only water around was in frozen form. As the Italians melted chunks of ice, the American Thomas Flyer flew past, followed by the French De Dion. But late that evening the Zust simultaneously overtook the Flyer and the De Dion, which were both stuck in the same snowdrift. All three crews working together managed to free the Thomas, but the heavy French car only sank in deeper. Not wanting to fall behind the Americans, the Italians left the French to their own devices and drove on. The De Dion caught up to them in Hudson, New York, where the three teams spent the night. George Schuster, the Flyer's mechanic, received a telegram informing him that his wife, Rose, was seriously ill. Schuster considered abandoning the race, but decided to stick with it one more day and see whether his wife's condition improved.

Sometime during the stay in Hudson, one of the cars—it's not clear which one—frightened a horse so badly that it broke its harness and galloped off. By the time the police got around to investigating the matter the following morning, the French and Americans were gone, leaving the Italians to pay the three-dollar fine.

On their first full day of travel, the American Thomas and Italian Zust took turns breaking a trail through what Scarfoglio called "this soft yet obstinate enemy," while the French De Dion tagged along behind. It was one of the few times that the crews would be moved by a spirit of cooperation rather than competition. When the snow was too deep on the roads, they broke down fences and drove across the fields.

"We shovel snow for miles and then we ride yards," sighed one of the De Dion's crew. "But," he added gamely, "we have only nineteen thousand, nine hundred and ninety-five miles yet to go."

The De Dion was far behind by the time the Zust and the Thomas reached Schenectady. The two leading cars decided to use the towpath alongside the Erie Canal, which was relatively clear of snow. Normally used only by mules towing canal boats, the path was treacherously narrow and nearly level with the water. A Buffalo, New York, newspaper warned, "A slip of the wheel and zip—you are in the canal bed and probably dead with the machine on top of you." A local car that was escorting them did, in fact, fall into the canal, injuring two men. But despite the danger, the Italians put on as much speed as possible—often forty or fifty miles an hour. The Americans had to match the reckless pace or fall behind.

Everyone knew that in Alaska and Siberia the cold would be a challenge, but they hadn't expected such brutal temperatures in New York. The biting wind cracked the exposed skin on the men's faces; when they were pushing the vehicle out of a drift and forgot their gloves, their hands stuck to the metal. Like most of today's cars, theirs were equipped with radiators to cool the water from the engine. Unfortunately, there was no decent antifreeze available, so if the crews stopped for very long, they had to drain the radiators to keep them from freezing and cracking.

Two days into the race, the weather began to warm a little and the snow turned to rain. It was not much of an improvement. In fact, in some ways it was worse; roads that had been waist-deep in snow were now knee-deep in mud and slush. "The chains wrapped around our tyres are no good," wrote the Zust's Scarfoglio. "The wheels churn up the water and race round on the slippery ground without taking any hold." He actually found himself longing for some snow to shovel.

The cars abandoned the towpath and returned to the main route. Unfortunately, the stretch of road that lay ahead of them was famous for being the worst in America—and that was saying a lot. Just outside of Geneva, New York, it took them through the middle of the Montezuma Swamp. At a spot appropriately called Dismal Hollow, the two front-runners found the road blocked by a snowdrift a hundred yards long and ten feet deep in spots. With the swamp on either side, they couldn't go around it.

According to the rules, the cars were to drive the entire distance under their own power. Fortunately, the commissioner general of the race, St. Chaffray, was no farther away than the front seat of the French De Dion. When he caught up with the Zust and the Flyer and saw their predicament, he promptly changed the rules and sent a man off to find a team of horses. The others sat there in the rain, brooding about the delay. "My heart is full of evil thoughts," wrote Sitori, the Zust's driver, "about the men who make the roads. . . . Italy is a poor country, but there are good roads in all directions and signs to tell the people where they lead to. Perhaps the roads in New York are not marked like that because the officials are ashamed to call them roads."

Only the De Dion's ever-optimistic Captain Hansen, the famous adventurer, was undaunted. "We're here for the night, boys," he said cheerfully, then launched into his rendition of a maddeningly repetitive Boy Scout song with the lyrics, "We're here because we're here because we're here because we're here," etc., set to the tune of "Auld Lang Syne."

As it turned out, they were there only a few hours before a farmer arrived with a team of six horses. Spurred on by the frightening roar of the engines, the animals dragged the cars to relatively solid, snow-free ground.

Despite the awful driving conditions, so far none of the leading autos had suffered a major breakdown. Both the Thomas and the Zust were equipped with chain drive, and both had been plagued by problems such as snapped chains and bent radius rods—adjustable metal bars that kept the chains tight—but nothing that couldn't be quickly repaired. Then, outside Rochester, the Italians had big trouble: a broken chain wheel, or sprocket. Though the three teams had agreed to enter Buffalo together and rest there for a day or two, the Thomas and the De Dion went on without the Zust, leaving its crew to labor over their vehicle, aided by Rochester's Italian community. At midnight Scarfoglio and his men set off again; the reporter noted that the Zust ran beautifully, "as if understanding that . . . the joy and pride of thousands of Italians depended upon it."

As soon as the Americans entered Buffalo in the Flyer, a worried George Schuster hurried home to check on his ailing wife, fortunately for the Thomas Company, Rose's condition had improved so much that the mechanic felt he didn't need to drop out. Just to be on the safe side, the company hired a backup mechanic, twenty-five-year-old George Miller.

The rest of the Flyer's crew and that of the De Dion spent a comfortable night in a hotel. In the morning, they set about making repairs and adjustments to their vehicles. Since the Thomas Company was headquartered in Buffalo, the Americans had plenty of expert help; the factory's mechanics replaced a cylinder and the front axle, strengthened the frame, and added an extra gas tank to the Flyer. St. Chaffray had the huge storage box on the back of the De Dion cut down, to reduce the weight.

The two teams were dismayed to learn that the Zust would not be joining them on the road. Angry at being abandoned, the Italians had driven straight through the night and were by then several hours in the lead. They had stopped in Buffalo just long enough to leave a message: "We will await you in San Francisco."

"The race," wrote the Flyer's George Schuster, "then became serious."

The three other entries were trailing by far more than a few hours. After the lumbering Protos blew out four tires in three days, the Germans realized they had to get rid of some weight. First they shipped six hundred pounds of supplies ahead to Chicago by rail. Then the car was accidentally lightened a bit more when the rearmost gas tank broke loose and fell off. "Thank God," cried Koeppen, "destiny is wiser than we are!" In Rochester, they lost a few more pounds; while the crew were eating, the crowd of race fans—presumably hungry for souvenirs—stole everything that wasn't tied down, including their extra shoes.

Even after these intentional *and* unintentional measures, the car was continually bogging down. Koeppen blamed the roads, not the car. "What terrible roads we have met! Why, if we were in Germany, we would be in Chicago now!" He was not happy about American gasoline, either; it clogged the gas lines, he claimed, and had to be filtered.

By February 17, the day the Thomas and the De Dion left Buffalo, the Germans were only 120 miles behind them and feeling optimistic. But just outside Buffalo, they blew their last good tire and made their grand entrance into the city driving on the rim.

A hundred miles to the east, the Frenchmen of the Moto-Bloc were trying to regain some ground after being laid up in Utica for most of a day with a broken fuel line. The happy-go-lucky Godard didn't seem particularly concerned; he preferred to be in the rear, he said.

But in truth, the Moto-Bloc wasn't bringing up the rear. Pons and the third French car, the little Sizaire-Naudin, were. On the very first day of the race, barely forty miles from the starting line, the axle cracked due to a flaw in the steel. Desperate to avoid dropping out as he had in the Peking–Paris race, Pons repaired it well enough to continue. He got another sixty miles before the Sizaire broke down beyond repair. (Years later, the manufacturer would claim that some other contestant had sabotaged the car by putting a pebble in the axle.)

Pons begged American automakers to provide him with a vehicle, vowing to drive twenty hours a day in order to catch the others, but no one was willing to back the man the *Times* called "a most unfortunate racer."

And what of the unofficial entry, the Werner? Lelouvier, who had proven to be a terrible driver, had a whole string of accidents in the first few days. After he slammed into a snowbank near Philadelphia, damaging the car badly, the rest of the crew demanded that he give up the wheel. The outraged Lelouvier gave up the whole enterprise and returned to New York. The crew drove on without him.

FEBRUARY 18–MARCH 3

The Italians in the Zust didn't stay out in front for long. Before the car reached Erie, the chain wheel (sprocket) broke three more times. While Haaga was repairing it, the Flyer and the De Dion recaptured the lead. It was a scenario that would play out again and again over the course of the race: One car gets well ahead of the others, the crew is elated, then disaster strikes.

But this time all the autos in the race were headed for disaster, and it had nothing to do with flat tires or broken chain wheels. The Midwest was about to be struck by the worst blizzard in years.

The cars made it across northwest Pennsylvania and Ohio with little trouble. It was cold—so cold that the Italians had to break their sandwiches in pieces with a hammer and defrost them on the radiator before they could eat them—but that had its advantages; the once-mucky roads were now hard as concrete.

Despite the Thomas crew's constant paranoia about being overtaken again by the Zust, there were some light moments. W. T. "Skipper" Williams, the pudgy correspondent who rode in the Flyer most of the way across the United States, recounted wryly, "One of the features of the race that always seemed to interest the public . . . was the desperate attempts made by THE TIMES reporter, clad in heavy coats, to clamber gracefully over the shovels, baggage, tires, and other impedimentia to his perch on the gasoline tank." The crowd rewarded him with cheers and shouts of "Bravo, fatty!" and "You'll lose that in Siberia!"

By the time the cars reached Indiana, the mood had turned grim. Conditions there were, according to the *Times,* "much worse than they will be in Alaska." The poetic Scarfoglio described the snow and ice as "fragments of glass, needles, and pins which penetrate our insufficiently covered faces" and the wind as "a gigantic sword, shaken by an unseen hand."

While Monty Roberts compared the Flyer's progress to Napoleon's retreat from Moscow, his boss, E. R. Thomas, safe and warm in Buffalo, was actually relishing the brutal weather. "It gives the Thomas Flyer, which is defending America, an opportunity to demonstrate its ability to overcome the worst possible conditions."

The trouble was, the Flyer *couldn't* overcome them. "The difficulty of automobile traveling," explained a reporter for the Chesterton, Indiana, *Tribune,* "lies in the way the snow packs under the body of the car, leaving the wheels to spin in the empty air." The Americans tried lightening the load to keep the car from pressing down into the snow, but removing all the baggage and even the portly Skipper Williams made no difference in coping with drifts ten feet deep. Finally, as much as they disliked doing it, Roberts and Schuster had to resort to using bona fide horsepower. After all, Commissioner General St. Chaffray himself had declared it legal back at Dismal Hollow. It took eight horses pulling together, plus the car's sixty-horsepower engine, to get the Flyer through the worst spots. In one day, the Americans laid out eighty dollars to hire teams and covered a distance of only fifteen miles.

Temperatures dipped as low as twenty-seven degrees below zero. The Italians removed the floorboards from the Zust so they could warm their feet on the exhaust pipe. One evening, worn out from trying to shovel through a snowdrift, they fell asleep in the car, only to discover in the morning that they were less than a mile from a sizable town.

Though the locals cheered the Zust on, most weren't willing to actually offer the Italians any assistance. Scarfoglio noted incredulously how they "candidly confess that they have smoothed the way for the Thomas because it was an American car; but they cannot move even a finger to help us. . . . It is a beautiful

The Thomas Flyer stuck in the snow.

example of patriotism; but it is a terrible thing for us." The crew did persuade one farmer to haul them out of a particularly daunting drift—for a price, of course.

Scarfoglio, Sitori, and Haaga, who had started out as wary strangers, were learning to pull together. The crew of the De Dion, meanwhile, were pulling apart. Though the adventurer Captain Hansen was normally an easygoing sort, he liked to be in charge. Unfortunately, so did the aristocratic St. Chaffray; the friction produced some heated exchanges. Hansen, who did none of the driving, felt free to criticize the commissioner general's abilities. He also accused St. Chaffray of making his crew do all the work but getting all the glory. The Frenchman retorted, "I am the nephew of the Marquis de Dion . . . and when I tell you to get out and push, you shall do so."

In Indiana, Hansen got into a more violent dispute—though not with St. Chaffray. He was attacked by a Swedish farmer who, the *Times* said, "mistook the gallant captain for a Norwegian sewing machine agent who had visited the village 10 years ago and separated the Swede, among other farmers, from certain sums of money." Farmer and adventurer grappled furiously, finally falling into a snowbank before Hansen managed to subdue the man using a wrestling hold he had learned as a miner in Siberia.

On February 22, Hansen was still putting up with St. Chaffray and still boasting to the press, "I shall enter the gates of Paris with the De Dion automobile winner of the Around-the-World race." Four days later, when the three leading cars finally made it to Chicago, the captain announced that he was bailing out and took a train east—but only as far as Buffalo. There he met with E. R. Thomas, who gave him a spot as navigator aboard the Flyer at a salary of a hundred dollars a month—a pittance compared to the money Hansen himself had riding on the race. He had wagered ten thousand rubles (around seven thousand dollars) that he would reach Paris by the 15th of June.

"One of the most astonishing features of the trip so far," wrote a poorly informed *Times* reporter, "is that no petty jealousies have developed among the crews of the cars." Not only did the De Dion suffer from the clash of personalities between St. Chaffray and Hansen, but its crew also had a scrap with the Italians of the Zust.

The Thomas Flyer enters Chicago.

Outside Chicago, the Zust had waited for the De Dion to catch up, with the understanding that the Italians would enter the city first. But St. Chaffray, feeling his country's honor was at stake, tried to take the lead. The polite procession turned into a mad dash, with the cars so close that their wheels rubbed together. At the last moment the Zust pulled ahead, to wild cheers from the city's Italian community.

The poetic Scarfoglio had not been impressed by the cities he had seen so far. "The American town is stamped with the brand of ugliness," he wrote. "They are rich in names which have been plundered from the geography and history of the world . . . their 'capitols,' 'pantheons,' and 'coliseums' are grotesque imitations of the great things of the past." But he found Chicago appealing because it made no attempt to mask its ugliness. "Chicago lives by smoked pig, boasts of it, and shows it in its dress like a good labourer. It is possible to like American towns when they are full of smoke, noisy with labour and the shrieks of steam sirens."

Despite his refined sensibilities, St. Chaffray also liked the city's raw energy. The French and Italians found another bit of common ground, as well. They both agreed that the American team had been guilty of cheating. During the layover in Buffalo, they said, the Thomas factory had practically rebuilt the Flyer, so it wasn't the same car that had started the race. The Americans had supposedly been towed long distances, too, both by horses and by a trolley car. What's more, the Flyer had been allowed to drive on the railroad and trolley tracks, while the De Dion and the Zust had to use the roads.

Though the third claim was true, the others were wildly exaggerated. The Flyer had been pulled through drifts, of course, but so had the other cars, and the changes made in Buffalo were relatively minor. E. R. Thomas peevishly replied, "The whole truth of the matter seems to be that the foreigners in the race are bad losers."

The Germans in the Protos, meanwhile, were having a feud of their own. When the press interviewed them, the focus was always on Lieutenant Koeppen, who was more outgoing than Knape or Maas and, unlike them, spoke a little English. Reporters referred to Koeppen as the driver, even though he couldn't drive, and called the others his "assistants," even though they were equal partners. "He loved to pose for the newspapers," said Maas, "and allow us to do all of the shoveling."

The two engineers finally handed the lieutenant an ultimatum: "Either you step down or we do." The trip, said Knape, had been all drudgery and no pleasure. "I had to laugh," Koeppen later wrote. "He really thought that this very first vehicle journey around the world was going to be a lark."

When the Protos reached Chicago on March 3, Knape and Maas bowed out. Koeppen hired a new driver/mechanic, O. W. Schneider, who had once served in the German army and, presumably, knew how to take orders.

Not far behind the Protos was the other French car, the Moto-Bloc, which was having problems of a different sort. In Wawaka, Indiana, the roguish Godard got a taste of his own medicine. He parked the car in a livery stable and in the morning discovered that all their equipment had been stolen. The police were no help. "Indeed," said Godard, "with our difficulty in making ourselves thoroughly understood, they seemed to regard us in as bad a light as if we were ourselves guilty." To add insult to injury, thirty miles down the road he was arrested for failing to pay a farmer he had hired to tow him. Though the Frenchman had a long history of shady dealings, this time it wasn't his fault; the farmer and his horses had never actually shown up.

Both Godard and Koeppen echoed the Italians' complaint that they were being treated unfairly by the locals. "They charge them with blocking their way," said the *Times*, "and filling up the road cleared by the cars that have gone before, and hampering the contest in many other ways."

While the Germans sat idle in Chicago, waiting for repairs to be made on the Protos, they received a telegram from the race committee. It contained one brief sentence, but that single sentence would have dire consequences for all the contestants; it would, in fact, drastically affect the course of the race and its outcome. Though there had been talk of shipping the cars across part of the United States by rail in order to get them to Alaska before the thaw, that notion was scrapped. They had to make it across the country by road. The telegram read, "ALL CARS MUST DRIVE TO SAN FRANCISCO UNDER THEIR OWN POWER."

The Flyer seeks a clearer route on railroad tracks in Indiana.

MARCH 4–20

The Americans weren't as disturbed as the other crews by the race committee's decision not to send the cars by rail. They were confident that they would reach San Francisco with a sizable lead. Whether or not they could make it to Alaska while the snow was still solid enough to drive on was another question altogether.

The Thomas had left Chicago on February 28, a day ahead of the Zust and the De Dion. Thanks to the conscientious Schuster—who had labored tirelessly over the car while the team's star, Monty Roberts, was being wined and dined—the Flyer had made it all the way across Iowa, struggling through the mud baths that passed for roads, with no mechanical problems more serious than a blowout.

Townsfolk along the route were so eager to cheer on their favorite that they were fooled by a phony Flyer. A young prankster named Willie Johnson borrowed his father's car, decked it out with American flags, and then recruited two other boys for his "crew." Wearing heavy winter coats and goggles, they drove into the town of Boone, Iowa. The population greeted them with wild enthusiasm—until they recognized the impostors.

When the real Flyer pulled into Omaha, Nebraska, on March 4, it was welcomed by a crowd of eighteen thousand—"the grandest reception we have had," said Roberts, "not excepting New York City." Captain Hansen came aboard there, replacing Skipper Williams, the *Times* reporter, who had had enough of bouncing about atop the car's fuel tank.

The Union Pacific Railroad, which began construction in 1865, had transformed Omaha almost overnight from a frontier town to a bona fide city. The residents threw a banquet for the American team, including Captain Hansen, at the Rome Hotel; Hansen, always happy to be in the limelight, spoke at length about his feud with St. Chaffray and about the problems they were likely to encounter in Siberia. Afterward, he and Monty Roberts visited the local roller rink, where they put a strain on their new status as teammates by engaging in a roller-skating race. Not surprisingly, since he was almost twenty years younger than the captain, Roberts won.

The sandy roads of the Great Plains were a big improvement over the muddy midwestern ones. The American team crossed Nebraska in only three days, following the same route used by wagon trains fifty years earlier. Some people still considered the covered wagon the best way of getting across the plains; the Flyer passed one on the way.

In Cheyenne, Wyoming, which billed itself as the "most wide-awake city in the West," the Flyer got another rousing reception, complete with lariat-twirling cowboys and a local cameraman who took moving pictures of the event. And the crew got another banquet, at which Monty Roberts revealed that he was retiring from the race in order to take another assignment—driving the only American entry, another Thomas Flyer, in France's famous Grand Prix. He announced that the diligent mechanic George Schuster would be taking over for him.

Monty Roberts welcomes Captain Hansen to the American team, after the Norwegian has a falling out with race commissioner and De Dion captain St. Chaffray.

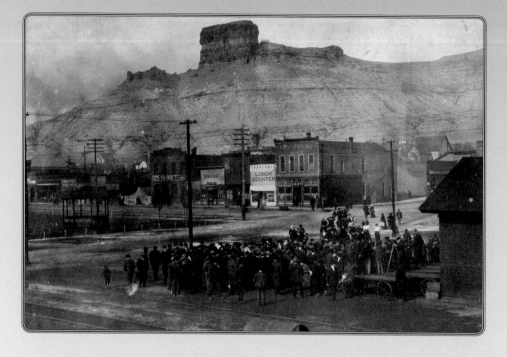

In western towns like Castlerock, Wyoming, motor cars were an unusual sight. Here the town comes out to take a look at the Thomas Flyer. Newspapers along the race route encouraged readers to treat the contestants politely, American or foreign.

Unfortunately for Schuster, the Thomas Company had other ideas. They had already designated a replacement driver—two, in fact. E. Linn Mathewson, a twenty-three-year-old Thomas dealer from Denver, would take the car as far as Ogden, Utah, where professional driver Harold Brinker would get behind the wheel. Schuster, though he had resented doing all the work while Monty Roberts got all the attention, had loyally kept his mouth shut, thinking his turn would come. Now he was being asked to take a backseat to Mathewson and Brinker. On the morning of March 9, as the crew prepared to leave Cheyenne, they discovered that Schuster was not in his hotel room. He had gone on strike.

The Americans had a backup mechanic now—George Miller, who had joined the crew in Buffalo. With him aboard, the Thomas Company's representatives felt they didn't really need Schuster. Monty Roberts convinced them that, without the skills of the original George, the Flyer would never make it to Paris. By the time Schuster turned up several hours later, the Thomas Company had agreed on a compromise: Brinker would drive the car only as far as San Francisco; Schuster would take it the rest of the way.

Captain Hansen, of course, wouldn't be doing any driving at all—except the backseat variety. Though he was little more than a passenger, the Americans put up with him; they expected his knowledge of the Arctic to prove useful when they reached Alaska and Siberia. Unfortunately, the captain insisted on offering his advice even when it wasn't wanted.

The crew of the Italian Zust had managed to avoid the personality clashes that plagued the others. According to Scarfoglio, they shared "one common sentiment, one common need—to push forward. For the rest we remain almost estranged and indifferent to each other. . . . Scarcely half a dozen words are exchanged in a day, and then they are words which belong to the journey and to the car. Sometimes Haaga sings to himself of his own country. Not so Sitori; he steers without uttering a word for hour after hour, like an automaton."

Their problems were mainly mechanical. In a little Iowa town, they had to replace a tire after someone—presumably a fan of the American car—stuck nails into it during the night. A little farther along, one of the wheels fell off. They repaired it with the help of "a body of ladies, who manage spanner [wrench] and hammer with skilful hands and do not disdain to cover themselves with grime and oil."

Near Marshalltown, Iowa, they passed a small settlement of Native Americans—presumably Mesquakie (Fox). Scarfoglio was dismayed at the tribe's wretched living conditions. "Civilization and brandy have reduced them to a very low level, and destroyed all the traditions of their race, all their customs, and compelled them, once the masters of this land, to shut themselves up in a 'reserved territory' which has scarcely the area of a handkerchief."

Heavy rains had turned the roads from mere mud baths to rivers of mud. "It is impossible to get on," said Scarfoglio, "unless the Zust is transformed into a motor-boat." The crew didn't manage that, but they did transform it into a train. The railroad not only allowed the Zust to drive along its tracks, it also provided the car with red and green railway lamps; word of its progress was telegraphed between stations as if it were a regular locomotive. Naturally, the car couldn't ride directly on the rails; instead, it jolted along over the wooden ties. After twenty-five miles of this, one of the car's leaf springs snapped. The Italians, already a day behind the Americans, lost another two days repairing it. Then the car slid into a ditch, breaking a gear; a replacement had to be shipped from Omaha. Yet another day lost.

The following day, the crew experienced a delay that was far more pleasant. As they sat eating in a restaurant, a group of young women crowded around them and the bravest asked Scarfoglio for a kiss. He obliged. "In the twinkle of an eye we were all seized and plunged into a seething whirlpool of arms and protruded lips. . . . It was the mammas who came to save us . . . barking out incomprehensible abuse. . . . The girls hesitated for another moment, then fled like a flock of sparrows."

The Italians had come to regard the Zust not as a mere machine, but as "the companion of our pilgrimage, the friend of our long wandering. And if it should die we should lament it as a lost friend." Just east of Granger, Wyoming, they came within an inch of killing off their friend—and themselves as well. They were racing along after dark, hoping to gain on the Thomas, when Sitori suddenly stomped on the brakes and jammed the car into reverse. "Then, mad with terror . . . he cries—'Quick, quick! Save yourself!'"

The crew scrambled out, to find that the front wheels were suspended in the air over a deep pit, where the railroad company had excavated gravel for its roadbed. Luckily, the car's axle had caught on the edge of the pit. After several hours of nerve-racking maneuvers with a tire jack and some discarded wood, they got the Zust back on solid ground.

Two days later, according to a report in the *Times*, the Zust encountered "the most exciting experience that has befallen any of the racing cars since leaving New York." As the auto started up a hill, it was surrounded by "not less than fifty wolves," snarling and snapping at them. "The crew attempted to pull away from the beasts, but the heavy roads and steep climb made this impossible. . . . Finally Scarfoglio and his companions got out their rifles and opened fire. . . .When the ammunition was all but exhausted the few remaining wolves dashed away into the timber."

It was certainly an exciting story. Fortunately for the Italians, not a word of it was true. "The most ferocious animal we had seen and killed," wrote Scarfoglio, "was a rabbit." The tale was concocted by some nameless—and shameless— newspaper reporter; knowing how eagerly readers were following the racers' adventures, he decided to give them what they wanted.

The crew of the De Dion now included a mechanic named Lascaris, who joined the car when Captain Hansen left. The Frenchmen weren't having any "exciting experiences," just one maddening mechanical malfunction after another, including a cracked frame, which cost them five days, and a broken driveshaft, which took two more days to repair. The high-strung St. Chaffray was convinced that the latter was the result of sabotage; he believed that a mechanic back in Paris, frustrated at not being chosen for the crew, had dropped a piece of metal in the transmission case. But he remained optimistic. Most of their troubles, he said, were merely a matter of bad luck, and luck had a way of turning. "When the leaders get their bad times," he wrote, "the De Dion will overhaul [overtake] them rapidly."

For the Germans of the Protos, bad luck had already arrived, in the form of the race committee's telegram. Lieutenant Koeppen's whole strategy had been based on the belief that any car that hadn't reached the West Coast by March 5 would be shipped by rail, and that all the entries would start for Alaska together. It hadn't mattered, then, that he was a full week behind the Thomas. Now, suddenly, it mattered very much.

That mistaken assumption of his had created another major problem: Figuring on taking the train to the West Coast, Koeppen had shipped all his extra parts, spare tires, and supplies ahead to Seattle. Hurriedly, he had them sent east again, to Omaha. On March 7, about the time the Thomas was leaving Nebraska, the Protos was just pulling out of Chicago. There was a gap of more than eight hundred miles between them, and not much time in which to close it.

The Frenchmen in the Moto-Bloc had been bringing up the rear since almost the start of the race. They had caught up with the Protos in Chicago, though, and after some fairly minor repairs, headed out again, several hours ahead of the German car. The irrepressible Godard—who had convinced reporters that he was in fact *Baron* Godard—had moved into fourth place at last.

He didn't keep it for long. Later that day, his car—which, like the Thomas and the Zust, had chain drive—threw up a stone that caught in the chain and broke one of the sprockets. The crew sat helpless in the middle of nowhere until the Protos came along and ignominiously towed them into the nearest town. "The succession of misfortunes has disheartened [Godard] greatly," said the *Times*, "but he declares he will go on to Paris if it takes him the whole year to complete the trip."

Unfortunately, the Frenchman's financial condition wasn't as strong as his determination. He still hadn't recovered all the equipment that had been stolen back in Indiana. And despite his new status as a "baron," he hadn't managed to con anyone into lending him money, as he had during the Peking–Paris race.

Finally he admitted, "I cannot continue to carry along the Motobloc on account of charges unforeseen and without end." On March 18, he loaded the car onto a freight train and shipped it to San Francisco, planning to somehow repair his car—and his money situation—there and then proceed to Alaska. Like the other contestants, he had gotten the race committee's telegram, but in typical Godard fashion he chose to ignore it. "I will win yet," he insisted. "The Motobloc will lead the procession into Paris."

MARCH 21–APRIL 7

On leaving Cheyenne, the Americans pushed themselves and the car harder than ever before. As anxious as they were to stay ahead of the Zust, they were even more anxious to reach San Francisco by March 23; if they did, they could make it to Seattle by train just in time to board a steamer that sailed for Alaska on the 26th. If they missed that ship, they would have to wait nearly a week for the next one.

The Thomas Flyer on a rough road in Nevada.

Though the crew were exhausted, the Flyer itself was holding up well, despite the rough roads and the snowdrifts it encountered in the Rocky Mountains. On several occasions the countershaft housings that supported the rear springs had cracked, but it hadn't caused any long delays.

When the car finally did have a major breakdown, it chose a desolate spot—the middle of Nevada, far from any town or telegraph line. Harold Brinker, the new driver who had taken the wheel in Ogden, gunned the car too hard as he was climbing a steep riverbank. The strain broke six teeth off the drive pinion—a large gear in the transmission—and cracked the transmission case.

Though Schuster would later generously call Brinker "a splendid driver," at the time he was surely muttering under his breath, "They should have let *me* drive." Renting a horse from a nearby ranch, he set out for Tonopah, sixty miles away, where he "borrowed" the necessary parts from the local doctor, who, fortunately, owned a Thomas.

The repairs set the Americans back nearly two days. They reached San Francisco on March 24. "It had taken us," wrote Schuster, "41 days, 8 hours, and

15 minutes to cross the country." Their time compared very favorably with the record, set in 1904, of just under thirty-three days. That drive had been made in midsummer. The only other car to cross during the winter had taken more than two hundred days to do it.

Though the Thomas crew had made remarkable time, especially considering the miserable conditions, it was one day too long. They couldn't hope to get to Seattle by the 26th and sail for Alaska on schedule. The *Times* felt it scarcely mattered, since "the attempt to cross Alaska at this late date is regarded here as foredoomed to failure." But, as Schuster pointed out, people had said the same thing about the trip across the United States.

The race committee now considered shipping the cars straight to Siberia, but decided to stick with the original plan of driving through Alaska and across the Bering Strait. Schuster, who was officially in charge at last, spent the next two days getting the Flyer in shape for Alaska and Siberia, strengthening the frame and replacing the springs, transmission, wheels, and drive chains.

Though Schuster was too busy to notice, San Francisco itself was undergoing a major makeover. Two years earlier it had been rocked by one of the strongest earthquakes ever recorded. Compared to similar disasters, the death toll was relatively small—seven hundred fatalities—but the quake and the resulting fires had wiped out twenty-eight thousand buildings. Though the city had made a remarkable recovery, it still had a long way to go; when St. Chaffray arrived, he would remark that "the capital of the West is like that of ancient Rome, as the greater part of the streets are glorious ruins."

As the crew of the Flyer were boarding a ship for Seattle on March 27, a young woman with a child handed the new team captain a baby slipper wrapped in an American flag. "Wear this," she said, "and you'll always have good luck." Schuster, feeling he would need all the luck he could get, tucked it inside his coat.

In Seattle, a new correspondent for the *Times*, George MacAdam, joined the American team. With George Miller, the new mechanic, that made three Georges. To avoid confusion, the others tagged the original George with the nickname "Schus."

ABOVE: *The Thomas Flyer racing through San Francisco with fans riding alongside on bicycles.*

LEFT: *The new crew of the Thomas, Captain Hansen and the three Georges: Miller, MacAdam, and the long-suffering Schuster.*

On April Fools' Day, they caught a steamer in Seattle for Valdez, Alaska. With a whole week of unaccustomed idleness facing him, Schus tried to relax by reading a book. It didn't do much to take his mind off the race; the book was *Peking to Paris: An Account of Prince Borghese's Journey Across Two Continents in a Motor-Car*, by Luigi Barzini, who had accompanied the winning driver in that contest. In any case, for most of the trip he was too seasick to read it.

Captain Hansen occupied himself with the carrier pigeons he had brought along, meaning to use them to send messages back to the newspaper office in Seattle. He attached a note to one of the birds and released it, but it was promptly attacked and killed by a flock of gulls. "It seemed an ill omen," wrote Schuster. "We released no more pigeons."

While the Flyer had been making its run for San Francisco, the Zust was still struggling through the Rocky Mountains. The Italian crew added one more item to their list of grievances against the Americans. The Union Pacific Railroad had let the Thomas team drive on the tracks through the Aspen Ridge tunnel, which saved them hours of travel time. But when the Italians requested the same privilege, the railroad turned them down. The Flyer's

The Thomas Flyer on a steamer to Valdez, Alaska.

tire chains had damaged the roadbed, they said, and no more cars would be allowed to use the tunnel.

When the Italians got word by telegraph that the Thomas car had broken down in Nevada, they suddenly had hopes of catching the Americans after all, and possibly even beating them to San Francisco. Just past Ogden, Utah, their hopes were dashed yet again by "a peculiar, inexplicable sound" coming from the differential. When they took the gearbox apart, they found lodged in it "a fine fat nail." Scarfoglio was sure it had been planted there by "some patriotic Yankee, who thus wished to ensure the victory of his own country."

The next day they discovered a serious crack in the car's frame. "Sitori had a moment of desperation on seeing the damage," wrote Scarfoglio. "He wished to retire from the race, but Haaga and I . . . persuaded him to remain." The Zust had to be hauled back to Ogden by train to be repaired.

On March 26, the Zust left Ogden for the second time. Since there was no chance now of overtaking the Americans, Scarfoglio and his crew decided on a detour to Los Angeles, where they expected to find better roads. Unfortunately, to get there they had to cross the arid Great Basin in Nevada and the Mojave Desert in California. After more than a month of battling snow and cold, they now had to cope with swirling sand and stifling heat.

Sitori and Haaga strike a pose in the desert.

67

Sitori proudly shows off the Italian team's next meal.

Ever since the discovery of gold in the Comstock Lode in 1858, mining towns had been springing up in Nevada, then fading away as the gold or silver ran out. The Italians passed through several of these boomtowns in various stages of development or decline. Goldfield, which was flourishing at the moment, "greeted us with banners and cheers. . . . They offered us a banquet in . . . a marvellous hotel all built of marble. . . . Never have I seen so many diamonds and precious stones as were poured out from full hands on the bosoms and heads of the ladies, or on the rings of the men. It was a crude display, which ended by inspiring disgust."

At Greenwater, California, they saw what happens when the boom goes bust. "The town has remained intact as though the inhabitants had gone away in the morning and would return in the evening." But in fact there were only seven residents left, living "like shipwrecked mariners in a desert island, recalling the glories of the mummified town around them, and re-reading the old numbers of the newspapers."

Beyond Greenwater lay the desolate landscape of Death Valley. To keep the Zust from sinking into the fine sand, the Italians tore an old tent into strips and laid the canvas under the wheels. "We seem to be in a furnace," complained Scarfoglio. To add to his misery, the ever-cheerful Haaga was "singing horrible German songs."

Once they reached the coast, the Zust ran "furiously, as a wild beast that is trying to run down an adversary." At last Scarfoglio had discovered a part of America that truly pleased him; he even went so far as to compare California to his beloved Italy. "After fifty days of torture we have found once more the scenes and the life which are dear to our eyes. . . . This is our own perfumed land, the remembrance of which had been dimmed by the mortal sadness of the country through which we have passed."

On April 4, the Zust arrived in San Francisco, where thousands of Italian Americans gave it a rousing welcome. Though the crew were grateful, they made it clear they were "in a race, not on a pleasure expedition, and cannot afford the time for festivities and entertainments." They had to get their automobile ready for the challenges to come.

"The De Dion car is on the Rockies," reported St. Chaffray on March 21. "Don't be proud of the fact." The French car had driven into a nasty spring snowstorm just outside Laramie, Wyoming. The wolves that had supposedly surrounded the Zust actually did turn up now and trailed the De Dion, probably more out of curiosity than hunger. The crew had more to fear from their fellow men. A guide they hired to show them the way to Ogden got them lost instead. As they searched for the right route, the mechanic, Autran, said, "It seems to me that something is burning in the car." He was right; their equipment was going up in smoke. "No matter how good the car," St. Chaffray commented wryly, "a fire is not pleasant in it." They managed to put out the flames with water from the radiator. The fire, it turned out, had been started by the guide's discarded cigarette.

Later, when the De Dion bogged down in a mud hole, St. Chaffray tried to enlist the help of two passing tramps. The strangers weren't interested. They were, however, very interested in the car's spare axle. Lascaris, the new crewman, spotted them trying to carry it off, presumably meaning to sell it. "He took out his revolver and gently told the robbers to help us for the sake of their lives," wrote St. Chaffray. "They helped strongly, and thanks to them the big car got out of mud."

Bad luck continued to plague the De Dion. In Death Valley, the team were engulfed in a blinding sandstorm. Like the Italians, they managed to creep along by laying pieces of an old tent under the car's wheels, but they couldn't see where they were going. When word of their plight reached the nearest town, a local man set out in a wagon to rescue them. His horses were apparently spooked by the sandstorm, for a second rescue party found him dead along the roadside, his neck broken.

Even in sunny California, the Frenchmen managed to encounter lousy weather. "Just what we expected," sighed St. Chaffray. "The New York to Paris racers cannot have a common sun or no trouble. It would be unfair."

They reached San Francisco on April 7, three days after the Zust. Like the Italians, they were greeted by an enthusiastic mob—a bit too enthusiastic, really. "As a sign of joy," wrote St. Chaffray, "and in order to preserve a souvenir of the event, they cut pieces off the canvas hood of the De Dion and took them away as relics."

The Germans in the Protos made good time after leaving Chicago; when the car entered Omaha it was only three days behind the De Dion. Though Lieutenant Koeppen was anxious to catch up, he took the time to learn a few driving skills in case anything should happen to Schneider, the driver he had hired in Chicago.

By the time they reached Wyoming, they were trailing the French car by only a single day. Then, near Rock Springs, as the Protos was crossing a railroad track, the flywheel struck one of the rails, breaking the drive shaft. To make matters worse, a train was bearing down on them. Koeppen and Schneider managed to push the heavy auto off the tracks just as the engine roared past.

After shipping the Protos to Ogden for repairs, Koeppen returned it to the exact spot where it had broken down. He was worried that, if he cut off even a few miles by taking the train, he might be disqualified. If he had known how things would turn out, he could have saved himself the trouble.

The lieutenant had two other major worries: He was running out of money and he was running out of time. The kaiser had granted him only six months' leave. He had been gone from Germany more than two months now, and had driven a mere twenty-five hundred miles—about one-fifth of the total driving distance. (Though the distance from New York to Paris was roughly twenty-one thousand miles, only about twelve thousand miles of it was on land.)

Leaving Schneider in charge of the car, he went ahead by train to Salt Lake City, where he arranged to draw money from his dwindling account in Berlin. "It is no race," said Schneider, "but an expense endurance test." On April 6, Koeppen rejoined the Protos—which in the meantime had broken down once more and been repaired—and they set off for Nevada.

But they had even more trouble getting out of Utah than the Zust and the De Dion had. The following day, the German car was aboard a train again, on its way back to Ogden. The lieutenant himself was on a different train, heading in the other direction. Two of the Protos's four cylinders had cracked, and the nearest replacement parts were in Seattle. Koeppen had gone to fetch them.

When the careless and cavalier Charles Godard arrived in San Francisco by train with his Moto-Bloc on March 24—only three hours after the Thomas Flyer got there—he still imagined that he could win. "This race across America," he said, "is merely a trifle compared to the journey through Alaska and Asia. I have some experience there and the advantages which the Thomas car enjoyed in this country will be mine when we get into Siberia."

He never got the chance to back up his boast. The rule was that all the cars must cross the country under their own power, and since the Moto-Bloc had gotten a lift from the railroad, it was disqualified. Godard's business partners instructed him to sell the car and return to France.

The "baron" had never been very good at following rules or instructions. He did sell the car—to a Nevada miner for 1,650 dollars—but he failed to pay the import duty on it, so he had U. S. customs officials after him. He was in trouble with the San Francisco police, too, for driving fifty miles per hour in a ten-miles-per-hour zone. Then an attorney showed up, demanding he pay the money he owed that farmer back in Iowa. By the time Godard boarded a ship for Europe, he was only too glad to be done with America. His opinion of the country could be summed up in a few words: "Bad roads, bad food, scant hospitality."

APRIL 8–APRIL 21

Because of submarine earthquakes and volcanic eruptions," reported the *Times* on April 8, "cable communication between Valdez and Seattle has been completely cut for the last ten days." This meant that neither the race committee nor the other entries knew exactly where the Thomas Flyer was or how it was faring.

In fact, the Americans had landed in Alaska that very day. The town of Valdez, which had sprung up during the Klondike gold rush of the 1890s, boasted a population of two thousand, plus two banks, three hotels, two newspapers, and electric lighting—but no automobiles and no roads worthy of the name.

"Ours was the first car ever seen there," wrote George Schuster, "and the inhabitants welcomed us with a band and parade." He was in no mood for festivities; he wanted to check out the condition of the Valdez–Fairbanks trail. One look convinced him of "the impossibility of driving through Alaska. Some drifts were higher than houses."

A few weeks earlier, he might have managed to drive over the frozen crust, but warmer weather had made the snow too soft. The only way to get a car through would be to dismantle it and haul the parts on sleds, at an estimated cost of ten thousand dollars, and even that was risky; earlier that same day, a horse and sleigh had fallen through the ice on a nearby river.

MacAdam, the reporter, noted that as the crew headed back to town, "a raven flashed across the trail and perched on a bare tree nearby. It might have croaked 'Nevermore,' and echoed the thoughts of the motorists." Schuster cabled a report to the race committee, which sent back these instructions: "RETURN TO SEATTLE ROUTE CHANGED TO GO SEATTLE TO VLADIVOSTOK."

When the Italians arrived in Seattle by ship on April 13, they were crushed to learn that they would be crossing neither Alaska nor the Bering Strait. "Thus ends the daring dream of our adventure," mourned the poetic Scarfoglio. "We are told that we should not have got beyond the Behring Strait [*sic*]. . . . That

LEFT: *A bear pulling a sled is one of the many sights Alaska offers the crew of the Thomas.*

BELOW: *A group of ladies in Valdez pose for a photo on the Thomas Flyer.*

would matter little. We had set out to perpetrate an act of splendid folly, not to open up a new way for men. We wished to be madmen, not pioneers. And we are disappointed in our madness."

To keep the playing field even, the Zust should have gone to Alaska and back, too. The Thomas Company said that wouldn't be necessary, as long as Scarfoglio and his crew let the American team keep the nine-day lead they had when they reached San Francisco. The Zust Company gratefully accepted those terms and agreed that its car would remain in Seattle until the Thomas returned, so they could ship out to Vladivostok together. But St. Chaffray, who arrived in Seattle at the same time as the Italians, wasn't willing to let the De Dion sit idle until the Americans returned. As commissioner general of the race, he had learned in advance that the Alaska leg had been canceled; as soon as he got to Seattle he booked passage on the next steamer to Japan. There he would aquire a Russian visa, catch a ship to Vladivostok, and get a big head start across Siberia.

Despite the Zust Company's promise that they would wait for the Flyer, Scarfoglio and his crew loaded their car on the same steamer taken by St. Chaffray. Either the Italians were unaware of the deal their sponsor had made, or they were so alarmed at the prospect of the French team taking the lead that they ignored it. Scarfoglio later claimed that they were just doing what the headquarters in Italy had instructed them to do.

As it happened, Lieutenant Koeppen was also in Seattle just then, but he couldn't join the French and Italians on the ship to Japan. His car was still back in Ogden, Utah—or so he thought—and still out of commission.

In his account of the race, Koeppen wrote that Germans in general like to make a plan and stick with it no matter what, and he was no exception. Imagine his dismay when, for the second time in a little over a month, he learned that the race committee had changed the rules. And for the second time, it put him in a very difficult position. Checking the schedules of steamship lines, he found that if he didn't get the car to Seattle by April 21, he would have to wait weeks for a ship to Siberia.

He asked the race committee to let him put the Protos on a westbound train. They turned him down. Determined to do his utmost for kaiser and country, Koeppen appealed to Commissioner General St. Chaffray, who, luckily, was close at hand. For some reason—perhaps to show that *he* was in charge of things—St. Chaffray overrode the committee's ruling and gave the lieutenant his approval. This reversal would have major repercussions.

Koeppen wired his driver at once, instructing him to ship the Protos to the coast by train. But Schneider was no longer in Ogden. He had gotten the car running again and driven it as far as Pocatello, Idaho, where it had another breakdown. Somehow the telegram reached him, and he put the crippled auto on a flatcar bound for Seattle. "In its present condition," noted one observer, "[it] looks like a pile of scrap iron."

Koeppen must have realized that he wasn't really playing fair; he told the *Times* that, though he still meant to take the car all the way to Paris, he should no longer be considered an official contestant. Somewhere between Seattle and Siberia, however, he would change his mind.

A sled carries gasoline for the cars through the snow-covered streets of Valdez, Alaska. The Thomas Flyer is the first automobile most residents have ever seen.

When the American team returned from their ill-fated jaunt to Alaska on April 10, they met up with Koeppen. Schuster, who came from German stock and understood the language, was forced to listen to the lieutenant's litany of troubles. The latest was that his driver had dropped out of the race, pleading illness. But, Schuster said, Koeppen "had telegraphed the Protos factory to have two factory men meet him in Vladivostok and was sailing there from Seattle on April 19. . . . I wanted to put our Thomas Flyer on the same ship but we lacked Russian visas, which we had expected to obtain in Alaska." Apparently the lieutenant had already obtained a Russian visa somehow.

To get theirs, the Americans had to apply to the Russian consul in Japan, as the French and Italians would do. The next ship for Yokohama sailed on April 21. And so it was that the Flyer, the first auto to arrive on the West Coast, was the last to leave.

APRIL 22–MAY 16

Throughout Europe and America, a large portion of the public was following the progress of the cars as avidly as today's sports buffs watch the World Series or March Madness or World Cup soccer. Newspapers carried detailed front-page reports on the race. In the window of the *Times* office hung a large map with flags that pinpointed the location of each auto. Immigrants gathered there to argue over whose country would win.

The New York City school system saw the contest as an entertaining way to teach geography. Preachers found it made good material for their sermons. "The reward will come to the men who patiently persevere in the face of gigantic obstacles," said one cleric. "This quality is essential also in the running of the race of life."

For the next week or so, race fans had to do without their daily dose of news. The contestants were all at sea, and since ship-to-shore radio wasn't widely used yet, they had no way of communicating with the mainland. All the press could do was speculate about what might happen once the cars reached Russia. The

The Thomas Flyer being loaded onto a boat to Japan.

fact that the racers would be traveling over an actual road—the "great" Russian post road—apparently fooled the *Times* into thinking that the going would be relatively easy. "No serious difficulty, as far as automobile travel in itself is concerned, is likely to be encountered in traversing Siberia," it reported—an opinion that would prove to be seriously misguided.

Actually, there was one interesting bit of race-related news: On the day the Thomas shipped out, the Seattle *Post-Intelligencer* announced that the unofficial entry, the Werner, had arrived in the city—minus Lelouvier, of course. Though the crew claimed they had driven all the way, witnesses in Oregon reported seeing the car aboard a train. The *Times* later learned that "the machine broke down at Columbus, Ohio, and was shipped on a flat car to St. Louis and there transferred to a box car, where it could not be seen."

In the first week of May, there was a sudden deluge of information that more than made up for the long drought. The most startling concerned St. Chaffray and the De Dion. When the commissioner general landed in Yokohama on April 30, he expected to find a letter of credit from his uncle, the Marquis de Dion, providing him with enough money to get to Paris. Instead he found a message informing him that the car was being withdrawn from the race.

The rationale given by the marquis was a rather lame one: The planned route through Siberia, he said, was so similar to the path of the Peking–Paris race that there was no point in driving it again. A more likely reason is that he didn't want to see the embarrassing outcome of the Peking–Paris contest repeated. Considering all the mechanical woes the car had suffered—plus the fact that the Thomas had a nine-day lead—he must have felt that the De Dion stood little chance of winning.

Like Godard, St. Chaffray was accustomed to ignoring instructions that didn't suit him. Scarfoglio, who had arrived on the same ship, described how "the three brave Frenchmen were wandering through Yokohama worried, hungry, but steadfast. . . . They will go on living by selling post cards, fortune telling, or anything, but will drive to Paris or die in the attempt."

Japan had begun trading with Europe and America only fifty years before, and according to Scarfoglio, this Western influence had robbed Yokohama, the major trading port, of whatever charm it had once had. It was "beautiful at night when one does not see the Europeans and their houses," but in daylight it seemed "a vulgar, banal city, without electric light, without tramways, without elegant women; a town which fills the soul with disgust."

The quickest way for the cars to get to Russia was to drive across Honshu— the largest of the islands that make up Japan—to the port of Tsuruga, which lies just across the Sea of Japan from Vladivostok. The foreigners spent eight frustrating days getting permission to cross the country. When the Zust finally hit the road again on May 6, "the De Dion car started with us, its occupants having miraculously overcome the financial difficulties." Presumably, St. Chaffray, like Lieutenant Koeppen, had dipped into his personal bank account.

The following day, the *Times* made an announcement that could be considered good or bad, depending on your point of view. For the Americans, it was good news: The race committee had upped their lead to fifteen days, supposedly to make up for the time they had lost going to Alaska.

Logically, the decision didn't make much sense. The Thomas Company had wasted a fair amount of money on the detour to Valdez, but no time was lost. The committee had already ruled that the cars were to meet up in Vladivostok and start across Siberia together—physically, anyway; technically, of course, the Flyer would still be in the lead. So, although Schuster complained that "our opponents had gained a week's start of us by sailing to Japan while we were still en route back from Alaska," in fact the Italians hadn't gained anything by jumping the gun. The Flyer was really entitled only to the nine-day lead it had when it reached San Francisco. (Actually, the Zust got to San Francisco *eleven* days after the Thomas, but only because it took the scenic route through Los Angeles.)

As far as Lieutenant Koeppen was concerned, the news was both good and bad. The good news was that the race committee had decided not to disqualify the Protos, since "there was some misunderstanding as to the right of the car to take a train after reaching Ogden, if necessary to catch a particular steamer to Alaska." The bad news was, the committee had slapped the German entry with a penalty of fifteen days—the estimated time it would have taken to get to Seattle under its own power.

While the Protos was headed directly to Vladivostok and the Thomas was en route to Yokohama, the Zust and the De Dion were creeping across Japan. After three months of constantly competing, the two teams managed to cooperate for a week or so. They shared the cost of a guide, helped each other out of mud holes, and took turns leading the way over roads that were far too narrow and across bamboo bridges that threatened to collapse beneath them; one did, in fact, fall to pieces a moment after they reached the far side. Somehow they made it across the island, arriving at the port of Tsuruga on May 12 with lives and vehicles intact. There they boarded a ship for Vladivostok.

The Flyer had just disembarked in Japan on May 12 several pounds lighter than when it left Seattle; its leather fenders had been cut completely away by the ship's Chinese crew, who used the material to put new soles on their sandals. The ship's carpenter fashioned a new set of fenders out of canvas.

TOP: *The Thomas Flyer crossing a bridge in Japan.*

BOTTOM: *Mechanic George Miller pouring water in the radiator as an interested Japanese crowd looks on.*

Unable to locate the Russian consul in Yokohama, the Americans went on to Kobe, where they obtained visas without all the waiting that had frustrated the French and Italians. They could have stayed on the same ship as far as Tsuruga and caught the steamer to Vladivostok from there. But the straight-arrow Schuster felt that, since the Zust and the De Dion had crossed Japan, the Flyer should, too.

The crew encountered the same problems with narrow roads and with bridges that were, in Schuster's words, "as springy as the best advertised mattress in the back of America's magazines." After each obstacle was conquered, they "climbed into the car to the cheering accompaniment of 'All aboard for Paris,' the established slogan on the Thomas car for all such occasions."

The Americans encountered one danger that the others had been spared. MacAdam, the *Times* reporter, recounted how, in Hachiman, they came upon a religious procession whose participants were "drunk with their fanatic enthusiasm. Whether they regarded the machine as some manifestation of evil spirits, or whatever else possessed them, they started to attack the car. . . . We made better time leaving Hachiman than over any other part of the road in Japan."

On May 15, the Americans reached Tsuruga. Thanks to the convoluted roads, "to cross the 90-mile wide island, we had driven 350 miles!" The following day, they set sail for Vladivostok, where the third—and at over eight thousand miles, by far the longest—leg of the race would begin.

MAY 17-JUNE 5

The decision not to send the cars across the Bering Strait caused some logistical nightmares. The Russian-owned Nobel Oil Company had put a lot of effort and money into placing caches of gasoline and oil along the original route. Between Moscow and Irkutsk, that was a relatively simple matter, since supplies could be shipped on the Trans-Siberian Railway, a 5,700-mile railroad line that had been under construction since 1891 (and wouldn't be completed until 1916). But to get drums of gas and oil into the desolate northern reaches of Siberia, the company had to use sleds drawn by dogs or reindeer. Now those caches were useless. A whole new string of supply depots had to be set up between Irkutsk and the Pacific Coast port of Vladivostok, the cars' new arrival point—a distance of nearly two thousand miles. By the time the Thomas Flyer landed in Siberia on May 18, Russian race officials had most of the gas and oil in place; unfortunately, they hadn't delivered any to Vladivostok yet.

There was little the race committee could do about the condition of the route itself. For much of the 5,300 miles from Vladivostok to Moscow, the cars would be traveling over the so-called "great Russian post road," which ran more or less parallel to the Trans-Siberian Railway and which was anything but great.

"In parts the road is accidentally good," reported one traveler, "due to the firmness of the binding materials which happened to be there, and rarely to the efforts of the road builder. It is not in a Russian to build a good road." Before the railroad came along, the post road had been the main artery of travel. Now it was in deplorable shape even in the best of weather; after three weeks of almost incessant rain, it had become a virtual swamp.

In the sparsely inhabited stretches—most of the route, in other words— there was little in the way of accommodations aside from the post houses, crude hostels that explorer Harry de Windt called "dens of filth and squalor."

But rotten roads and vermin-infested sleeping quarters promised to be the least of the contestants' worries. "Most disquieting rumors have reached us," wrote MacAdam, the *Times* correspondent, "of robber bands between here and Harbin." These bands, made up of nomadic warriors called the Chungese, had been attacking towns in southeastern Siberia and Manchuria. "They had heard of the projected trip of the rich automobilists through the country, and believed a good ransom could be secured by their capture. Added to the other difficulties . . . this indeed makes a pleasing prospect."

There were, luckily, a couple of genuinely pleasing prospects, in the form of prizes. For years, officials of the Trans-Siberian Railway had been considering a branch line that would run northeast from Irkutsk all the way to the Bering Strait. If cars could conquer the forbidding landscape, they reasoned, it would make the idea of building a railroad across it more feasible. Back when the plan was to take the cars across the Bering Strait, the railway had announced a prize of a thousand dollars, to be given to the first auto to reach Irkutsk by way of northern Siberia. Now that the route had changed, the prize was still being offered, but it would go to the first car to travel from Vladivostok to Chita, a city about four hundred miles east of Irkutsk.

In addition, the *Times* reported, the Russian Automobile Club, "inspired by the keen interest of the Russian nobility in the contest," would award a prize of equal value to the first entry to arrive in St. Petersburg, then the country's capital city.

The crew of the Flyer had every expectation of taking both prizes. "The car is in splendid shape," declared newspaperman MacAdam, "and . . . will be able to give as good an account of itself in Siberia as it did in America."

Koeppen was, if not exactly confident, at least very determined. "As a German officer," wrote MacAdam, "Lieut. Koeppen's professional honor requires him to contest the race to the bitter end." The Protos Company had "arranged to provide him with all the necessary sinews of war, including two expert German chauffers, who were sent on to Vladivostok from Berlin."

Koeppen wasn't impressed with his new teammates, Caspar Neuberger and Robert Fuchs; nevertheless, he put them to work at once. Despite his distaste for changing things, the lieutenant had them give the Protos a complete makeover. Having learned the hard way the disadvantages of a heavy vehicle, he had every pound of dead weight stripped away. He shipped nearly all the cold-weather gear and the spare parts ahead by train   and, he admitted, "we never again saw most of them."

With admirable foresight, he also bought most of the gasoline stocked by the German department store in Vladivostok and sent it ahead to various locations on the route, along with a supply of tires.

The French team didn't need to worry about gas or tires; they no longer had a car. The Marquis de Dion had sold the vehicle out from under them, to a Chinese auto fancier. Though his two crewmen gave up and bought train tickets home,

St. Chaffray had other plans. For him, as for Lieutenant Koeppen, this was not a mere sporting contest. His pride, both as a gentleman and as a representative of his country, was at stake. The race had been his idea, after all, and he was its commissioner general. How would it look if he dropped out?

In his desperation to continue, he resorted to some distinctly ungentlemanly tactics: He bought up all the gasoline he could find, not only in Vladivostok, but in Harbin, Manchuria, the next city on the route. Then he called a meeting with the American and Italian teams and made them an offer they couldn't refuse: "There is no petrol; there are no means of getting any. What there was is in my possession, and I offer it to the car which will agree to take me on board." He hadn't included Koeppen in the deal because he didn't feel the Protos stood any chance of winning. "He further said," wrote MacAdam, "that it would not look well for a Frenchman to ride on a German machine."

Schuster and Scarfoglio indignantly refused, even though it meant they might have to wait for the next shipment of gasoline from Japan. The good luck charm Schuster had received back in San Francisco must have been working, because the next day he found a source of gas that St. Chaffray had overlooked: A number of American boats were moored in the harbor, and each contributed a little fuel to the Flyer. The German department store and the local pharmacy also had some gas left, though Schuster had to pay the exorbitant price of $1.25 a gallon. He ended up with a supply large enough to allow him to send some on ahead for later use.

Defeated, St. Chaffray caught the train to Paris. But before he left, he had a fit of generosity and gave all the fuel he had cornered to the Italian team. Not that it did them any good. For reasons that Scarfoglio never explained, the Zust had been pulled—at least temporarily—from the race. Apparently, the car's backers had withdrawn their financial support and the Zust Company was scrambling to find more funds. According to Koeppen, the company had actually sold the car to a Russian sportsman, but if so, the man never came to claim it. While the American and German teams made preparations to leave, the Italians sat idle, too broke and disheartened to continue, uncertain what would become of them or their car.

A STOP AT A RUSSIAN MILITARY POST

The Thomas Flyer at a Russian outpost near Vladivostok, shortly after it arrived from the United States.

Vladivostok was hardly the ideal city in which to be stranded. Russia's only large port on the Pacific and the eastern terminus of the Trans-Siberian Railway, it was also the military headquarters for much of Siberia and for part of Manchuria, a province of China that was under Russia's control. The city's population of 120,000 was made up largely of soldiers and foreign merchants.

Not surprisingly, Scarfoglio didn't like it much. "Vladivostock was intended to be a metropolis. . . . it has become an enormous, useless barrack, full of wounded soldiers, of scintillating [flashy] officers, and Chinese thieves, and mud."

The Germans were ready to depart on the morning of April 22. The Americans thought they were, too. Schuster wrote, "I tucked the little flag and the baby shoe given me in San Francisco into my breast pocket and started the Thomas." But if the talisman really had dispensed good luck, it had run out. The Flyer's clutch (the device that transfers power from the engine to the transmission) was slipping so badly that the car could barely move.

Koeppen's patience had run out, too. The seemingly incessant rain had let up for the moment, and he didn't want to waste the good weather. Disregarding the race committee's instructions, he took off without the Thomas.

By the time Schuster and Miller fixed the clutch, they were two hours behind. The road, wrote MacAdam, "was a streak of mud as far as the eye could reach." Bringing up the rear actually proved an advantage; they could see all the spots where the Germans had bogged down, and detour around them.

They had gone no more than twenty miles before they came upon the Protos, "so deep in the mud that only the tops of the rear wheels showed." Schuster would have left the Germans to their fate, but Captain Hansen felt that would be unsportsmanlike. The American team hooked a tow rope to the other car and, with the Flyer's powerful engine, muscled it out of the mire. "Lieutenant Koeppen uncorked a bottle of champagne," said Schuster, "and poured drinks by way of thanks for what he called 'a gallant, comradely act.'"

Considering all the other supplies he sent on ahead, it seems curious that Koeppen should keep a bottle of champagne. It may have been a way to avoid drinking contaminated water. Schuster said that, for the same reason, his team took along a supply of cognac, vodka, and Japanese carbonated water. Presumably, the designated driver drank the carbonated water.

Several hours later, it was the Thomas's turn to get stuck, but there was no Protos around to help; in an effort to avoid the mud, Koeppen had taken a different route. Captain Hansen, who spoke several Siberian dialects, volunteered to go for help. He returned in an hour or so with forty soldiers from an army post a few miles away; in no time they had the Flyer back on solid ground—as solid as the ground got, anyway.

Both teams quickly realized that their best bet was to drive along the roadbed of the Trans-Siberian Railway. But that, too, had its hazards. The tracks were so narrow that, if they drove with the left wheels inside the rails, the right wheels had to tread a very narrow path. Turn too far one way and the spikes that held down the rails chewed up the wheels; too far the other way and they dropped off the end of the wooden ties. The Germans removed one fender so they could see the position of the wheel better. The Americans wound the tires on the right side with heavy cord to protect them. Even so, they wore out four tires in the space of 150 miles.

That, however, was a minor inconvenience. Since they hadn't gotten permission to use the tracks, their main fear was meeting an oncoming train. "The only place where we could turn out were at stations and at road crossings, miles apart," reported MacAdam, "and the nervous strain of listening for trains ahead and behind us was most exhausting." Six days out of Vladivostok, as they were driving through a series of mountain tunnels, "we heard a whistle ahead. There was no place to get off the track in sight, and we started on a wild run through a tunnel in the hope of getting away on the other side." But a flagman appeared, waving frantically for them to clear the track. "We were able to back up at the very entrance of the tunnel in a space just wide enough to allow the train to pass. An instant later the St. Petersburg Express passed us."

For the next thousand miles or so, the race route followed the Chinese Eastern Railway, a branch of the Trans-Siberian that cut across Manchuria. Just before they entered the Chinese province, the Thomas team stopped in the Russian border town of Pogranichnaya. The army regiment there warned Schuster again that "the country was infested with Chinese brigands, well mounted and armed. . . . No travelers were safe unless they paid tribute or were well armed."

WAITING FOR RIGHT OF WAY AT GOLENK ON THE TRANS-SIBERIAN RAILWAY

The Thomas Flyer waiting for the right-of-way along the Trans-Siberian Railway.

RIGHT: *The Thomas Flyer slips off the tracks and narrowly misses a plunge down a steep embankment.*

BELOW: *The Flyer gets a little help along a stretch of the Trans-Siberian Railway.*

A CLOSE CALL A SLIDE OFF THE TRACK ON A HIGH EMBANKME

THE THOMAS CROSSING TEMPORARY TRACKS ON HAND CARS

In the morning, the Americans set out for the city of Harbin, driving as usual not on the roads but on the tracks. "Four miles inside the Manchurian border," Schuster wrote, "there came a cracking sound from our transmission, and the car stopped. Six teeth were broken off the driving pinion [gear], and oil was leaking from a six-inch crack in the transmission case." It was a carbon copy of the breakdown they'd had back in Utah, and this time Schuster had nobody to blame but himself.

There was no habitation or help for miles in any direction. After the team pushed the Flyer off the tracks, Schuster and MacAdam, the reporter, walked the fifteen miles back to Pogranichnaya. While Schuster caught a train for Harbin, where his spare parts were being held, MacAdam bought up a supply of food and then hitched a ride on a railway handcar back to the desolate spot where the disabled Flyer sat.

Knowing they were in for a long wait, MacAdam, Miller, and Hansen set up a framework of old railroad ties and draped rubber coats and pieces of canvas over it to form a tent. Because of the threat of bandits, the men took turns standing guard. "The TIMES's correspondent drew the first watch," wrote MacAdam.

It was then, as he sat scribbling in his notebook, shivering in the cold night air and listening to the melancholy frog chorus, that he heard the alarming sound of footsteps crunching on the gravel of the railroad bed. Assuming the worst—that the approaching men were bandits—he got to his feet and cocked his rifle, only to discover, as the visitors moved forward into the firelight, that they were "two soldiers sent by the commandant of the Pogranitchnaya [sic] garrison. . . . The soldiers quickly extinguished the camp fire, saying it would be too good a mark for the [Chungese]."

The site, which the men dubbed Camp Hard Luck, "became a scenic feature of the railroad. The windows of all the trains were filled with people looking at the Paris racers." The days were sweltering, the nights near freezing. Their shabby tent afforded little protection from the rain; a hailstorm threatened to flatten it completely. After five miserable days, Schuster returned at last with the parts they needed to repair the transmission—for the moment, anyway.

Thanks to the Flyer's breakdown, the Germans now had a 150-mile lead. They were still rattling along on the ties of the Chinese Eastern Railway rather than risking the muddy roads. But after the Protos caused several trains to be delayed and narrowly escaped colliding with another one, railway officials declared that the cars could no longer travel on the tracks.

The decision not only slowed the Germans down considerably, it nearly took them out of the race altogether. Back on the road, they were crossing a wooden bridge over a deep ravine when the new driver, Neuberger, heard a sharp snap. He reached a foot out for the brake pedal, meaning to stop and investigate. Instead, he hit the accelerator and the Protos lunged forward. The mistake was a fortunate one; just as they reached the other side, the bridge collapsed.

Two days out of Harbin, the German car slid into a ditch and overturned. As the crew, slathered in mud, struggled to free it, a representative of the Russian royal family turned up. Grand Duke Serge Mikhailovich, an auto enthusiast and member of the race committee, had been heading east by train and had instructed the engineer to stop if he spotted any of the entries. When the grand duke saw the Protos wallowing in the mire, he reversed the railroad company's ruling on the spot; the cars would now be allowed to drive on the tracks, provided they carried a railroad official with them.

The Germans made far better time after that. They arrived in Harbin on June 4, five days ahead of the Thomas team. Though it was technically in China, Harbin had been built by Russians only eight years earlier, to serve as a major stop on the railway. It looked quite prosperous, with large stone buildings and palatial mansions that housed merchants and railroad officials. Even Scarfoglio would have been impressed.

Unfortunately, he and the rest of the Zust crew were still stuck in Vladivostok, waiting for their sponsors to decide their fate. On May 28, they finally received word from home. It was bad news. "[Sitori] has been recalled to Italy for some silly reason by the Zust people," Scarfoglio complained. (According to the *Times*, the manufacturer wanted Sitori's help getting a car ready for a different race.) "He can scarcely restrain his grief. . . . So Haaga and I remain more than ever

MacAdam on the left and Miller on the right at Camp Hard Luck in Manchuria.

alone and sad in this sad country. We sleep together in one room, always go out together arm-in-arm, eat together at the same table, owing to an instinctive fear that one may be snatched away and leave the other alone."

On June 2, the *Times* printed a letter from the Zust Company. "We notice that several European papers have published a statement that we have withdrawn our car from the New York to Paris contest," it read. "This is absolutely false." The company, it seemed, had "reached an arrangement with a prominent Italian sportsman who, rather than see the Italian car withdrawn, has agreed to undertake half the expense."

By June 5, the Italian team had the funds they needed to get on the road again. Scarfoglio was overjoyed to finally bid farewell to Vladivostok, "the wretched town where I have spent twenty-two days, where I have suffered weariness and solitude, and which I have so many times mentally despatched to the devil."

JUNE 6–JUNE 25

Though the railroad had assigned a man to accompany the Protos as agreed, the Germans—still in the lead—decided to stay off the tracks for a while;

The Thomas Flyer fords a river in Mongolia. In some places there were no bridges or ferries to aid the cars in water crossings, so the drivers made a flying start, hoping their car's momentum would carry them safely across.

the constant jolting had repeatedly broken the car's leaf-spring suspension. Instead, they drove right across the plains. There were no roads as such, but the land had flattened and dried out so much that it made for far better driving than most of the highways they'd encountered so far.

There were also, unfortunately, very few bridges. As they were trying to ford a stream by the dubious method of plunging into it at a high speed, the leaf springs broke yet again. With all its considerable weight resting on the rear axle, the Protos wouldn't budge. The railroad employee offered to walk to the nearest station for help.

When night began to fall and the man hadn't returned, Lieutenant Koeppen rather foolishly set out to find him, only to end up lost himself. After wandering about in the dark for seven hours, he began to despair. Then he heard a band of men on horseback approaching. Assuming they were Russian soldiers, he hailed them.

They were, in fact, the Chungese bandits the contestants had been warned against—half a dozen of them. Communicating mainly through sign language, they offered to take him to the railway station, for a price. Koeppen suspected that once they learned he was carrying two thousand rubles in cash, they would simply rob him—or perhaps kill him and *then* rob him. Luckily he was also carrying a revolver.

In one account of the incident, Koeppen says that merely firing into the air scared off the outlaws. A later version is more colorful: As the brigands close in on him he shoots "without warning one of the Chungese out of the saddle. He falls and is caught by his companion. I fire a second and third shot into the air. Like a miracle they stop. I can see the fear in their yellow faces. I fire a fourth shot, a fifth. 'Can these cursed Europeans shoot forever?' they must think. They choose the better part of valor—discretion. . . . As suddenly as they came, they disappear into the morning fog." Koeppen had survived the encounter, he said, by applying the same tactic he used in the race: Get ahead of your opponent.

Two hours later, the lieutenant stumbled upon the railroad station, which was headquarters for a small garrison of soldiers. A group of them rode out and dragged the Protos from the stream. In return, the Germans let the stationmaster's sister ride in the car as far as the next station.

Koeppen now "pushed the car to the limit," according to the *Times*. "The Protos stopped at night . . . only long enough for the crew to get three or four hours' sleep, and was then off again." Though the suspension gave out once more—it was the tenth time since leaving Vladivostok—the Germans kept the lead all the way to Chita and claimed the Trans-Siberian Railway's thousand-dollar prize.

Chita, the capital of the mountainous Trans Baikal region (the area east of Lake Baikal), was an attractive town of neat white houses; unfortunately, the climate was very dry, and when a wind came up, it sent sand swirling through the streets, leaving behind an ankle-deep layer of the stuff. Many of the twelve thousand or so townspeople were exiles, banished to Siberia because of their political beliefs.

The original residents were the Tungus, a fiercely self-reliant nomadic people who survived by trapping and herding reindeer. Some still lived in the area, in dwellings constructed of poles and reindeer skins, but, like Native Americans, they saw their way of life beginning to disappear as Siberia became more settled.

The fact that the Flyer was now in second place was a constant source of irritation for Schuster. Though the breakdown at Camp Hard Luck could hardly be considered his fault, he felt personally responsible. After all, when Monty was in charge, they had managed to stay in the lead, despite all sorts of mechanical problems.

Like Koeppen, Schuster was pushing his car and his crew too hard, but he pushed himself even harder. The Germans managed to put in twenty-hour days only because they switched drivers; Schuster refused to turn over the wheel to anyone else. Naturally, their leader's insistence on doing everything *his* way grated on the rest of the crew, and particularly on Captain Hansen, who had quarreled incessantly with St. Chaffray over that same issue. Hansen already had reason to be in a foul mood: It was the middle of June and they were still a long way from Paris, which meant the captain had lost his seven-thousand-dollar wager that he would reach the finish line by June 15.

When Hansen balked at following some order, Schuster threatened to fire him. "You do that," replied Hansen, "and I will put a bullet through you." George Miller stepped in and backed up his boss. "If there is any shooting," he said, "you will not be the only one doing it, Cap."

The tension aboard the Flyer wasn't helped any by the disturbing news, reported in the *Times*, that the Thomas Company had received "several threatening letters . . . saying that an attempt would be made to damage its automobile."

The dearth of decent meals and accommodations further dampened the crew's spirits. "At home," wrote Schuster, "we could always count on food and a clean hotel at the end of a journey. In Manchuria and Siberia there was neither, the hotels being bug-ridden hovels that made one glad to sleep on the veranda, in stables, in wagons, on the ground—anywhere, in fact, but under the roof of a house. Food was as bad, the staple article of diet apparently being a coarse black

George Miller works while a Russian man enjoys a rest on the fender of the Thomas.

bread, the crust of which could be eaten but the inside of which was absolutely indigestible."

By the time the Americans reached Chita on June 17, they had cut the Protos's lead to three days. They continued to narrow the gap, driving relentlessly most of the day, sleeping a few hours on the cold, hard floor of some post house without overcoats or blankets to cover them, and then pressing on.

Despite the Russian race committee's efforts, the team often had trouble finding gas and oil. Desperate for something to lubricate the sprockets and chains and the hastily repaired transmission, Schuster bought up forty pounds of Vaseline. (The petroleum by-product was widely used as a medicinal salve.) Later, he resorted to using beef fat, which led Miller to complain, "This car smells like a scavenger's wagon."

On June 21, the Thomas finally caught up with the Protos—for a few minutes, anyway. The Germans had reached Lake Baikal the day before and found that they could save considerable time by taking a ferry across the lake. Since the road was washed out, the only way of getting to the ferry was by train. They had just loaded the Protos onto a flatcar when the Flyer and its haggard crew pulled up.

Unfortunately, the train was scheduled to leave in four minutes—not nearly enough time for the Americans to get their car aboard. They could only watch in frustration as the flatcar bearing the Protos pulled away. Then they sat and waited for the next train, which wouldn't arrive for twelve long hours. At least it gave Schuster a chance to get some sleep and the others a chance to get a good look at the astounding Lake Baikal, which is nearly four hundred miles long and fifty miles wide and, in places, a mile deep—in fact, the deepest lake in the world.

While the Protos and the Thomas were competing for the lead, the Italians were enduring what Scarfoglio called "a complication of catastrophes." They had opted to take the roads rather than the railroad tracks, and at first it seemed like a good choice; they were making far better time than the Protos or the Flyer had. Then, two days out of Vladivostok, they came upon an area where the flood-swollen Ussuri River had broken down the dikes built to contain it.

"The plain all round us was like an immense lake," wrote Scarfoglio. As night descended and the rain continued to fall, the water slowly rose until it threatened to engulf the Zust. "We dismounted the magneto and the carburettor so that the water should not penetrate them. . . . On the water all around us are floating the bodies of drowned cattle, some of which collect around the car."

Huddled together atop boxes and suitcases, the men stripped down, preparing to swim through the debris and the dead cattle to try to find help. But as dawn came, they saw that the flood had started to subside. By noon, they were struggling westward again. "There is another stretch of flooded country ahead of us," said Scarfoglio. "But, forward! and come what may."

At times, the young poet-journalist actually seemed to welcome the prospect of difficulty and danger. He claimed that, when he and Haaga were warned about the outlaw gangs ahead, "this announcement afforded us a certain amount of pleasure. We have been traveling for a long time across the world in search of a warlike adventure and to-day when the opportunity of one is offered we cannot feel otherwise than gratified."

Still, some of the tales told about the bloodthirsty Chungese gave him pause: "There are red-hot irons waiting for us, melted lead for our ears, dissections to be conducted with real ability and wisely directed slowness. . . . There are, moreover, tigers . . . as numerous as the sands of the sea, tigers that have been made voracious by two years of famine." As they approached Manchuria, they were, he said, "feeling a little emotion, which was, of course, a long, long way removed from fear."

They met no tigers, and the only brigand they encountered was a telegraph operator who refused to send one of Scarfoglio's dispatches because he was convinced that it was written in secret code; he had never before encountered the Italian language.

The state of the roads in Manchuria was so deplorable that finally, like the other two teams, the Italians chose the teeth-rattling torture of driving over the railroad ties. And like the others they inevitably met an oncoming train and had nowhere to pull off. The situation turned even more serious when Scarfoglio saw smoke and flames pouring from the Zust's engine compartment. "Haaga and I dismount, forgetting the other danger in the presence of this more pressing one. We take off the bonnet [hood] and throw on clothes and furs to extinguish the flames. . . . Ah! save it, save it!"

Though they got the fire out before it did much damage, it would hardly have mattered if the engineer hadn't managed to bring the train to a screeching halt "a hundred paces away."

So relieved were they to have survived, they broke out a bottle of champagne. Aside from that one luxury item, their supply of food and drink was reaching rock bottom. Their supper that night consisted of "two alleged Frankfort sausages, corned beef which resembles shoe leather, and six sardines . . . fished up from the depths of an old tin, in which they were swimming about . . . in the company of two dead locusts."

They could buy food from the locals, of course, but there wasn't much to choose from. Scarfoglio griped about how monotonous it was "to feed eternally on bread, tea, and eggs—on eggs, tea, and bread—on bread, eggs, and tea."

In the miserable week that followed, the Italians bogged down in the mud so badly that it took twenty Russian soldiers to pry them out; they spent three days repairing a broken spring; the chassis cracked yet again; they struck a rock with

One of the few reliable foods on the Asian portion of the route was eggs, which the motorists grew tired of eating. Here George Schuster buys an egg from a Mongolian girl.

the gas tank, putting a hole in it; and they lost a wheel. This was not adventure, Scarfoglio complained, it was merely "disasters, disasters without end!"

When they reached Harbin on June 15, they were trailing the Thomas by a mere three days. By the time they finally got out of Manchuria, they were ten days behind the Americans.

JUNE 26–JULY 8

On the western side of Lake Baikal lay Irkutsk, the largest city in Siberia. Its diverse population, which included settlers, miners, exiles, and fur traders, enjoyed such cultural amenities as circuses, dances, and concerts. One crucial thing the city lacked, though, was a decent supply of gasoline. The Germans spent several hours trying to locate enough fuel for their auto; the Americans, who arrived just after the Protos left, had even more trouble.

For the next week, the Thomas and the Protos were basically running neck and neck. Neither crew dared stop anywhere for long, for fear of losing the lead or a chance at it. When they managed to catch a few hours' sleep, the *Times* reported, their dreams were "troubled by the image of a flying foe who would keep just beyond reach, or who was forever dogging at one's heels."

They didn't have so many rickety bridges to cope with now. The larger rivers could be crossed by ferry; most consisted of a large flatboat attached to a cable and powered by the current. But the teams had as bad luck with ferries as they'd had with bridges. At one river crossing, the Germans learned that the boat had been swamped by the current and wasn't operating. On the suggestion of the local villagers, logs were lashed to the bottom and sides of the Protos, turning it into a sort of raft, which four horses then towed across the river.

The locals were just as eager to help the Americans—a little too eager, in fact. "Half the people of one village," wrote MacAdam, "insisted on getting aboard a ferryboat with the Thomas car. The weight was so great that the boat sank and stuck on the bottom. The villagers swam off, set to work with a will, and towed the boat to the shore, but valuable hours had been lost."

These villagers were probably immigrants from western Russia. The original inhabitants of the area were the Buriat people. Like the Tungus, they were traditionally nomadic, but they had adapted better to the changes brought by the railroad and by the influx of exiles and other settlers. Many Buriats had begun raising crops and cattle. Though most practiced Buddhism, they retained some of their ancient beliefs; the trees in the vicinity were decked with fluttering scraps of cloth, tied there to frighten off evil spirits.

Schuster had finally admitted that he couldn't do all the driving himself. "We had decided not to rest until we caught up with the Protos," he said, "so Miller relieved me at driving, while I slept. We drove all night, two nights." They installed a heavy strap across the passenger seat "so that one of us could sleep in it while the other drove. It was perhaps the first use of a 'seat belt' in an automobile."

Technically, of course, the Thomas team had a thirty-day advantage—their fifteen-day bonus for the side trip to Alaska, plus the fifteen-day penalty incurred by the Germans for shipping the Protos by rail. But neither the Flyer's crew nor its manufacturer wanted to win on a technicality. They wanted their car to be the undisputed winner, and that meant beating the Protos to Paris.

Schuster was reluctant to really pour on the speed, though, for fear the car's gears would break again. He had ordered a whole new transmission from Buffalo, but it was being shipped to Omsk, five hundred miles down the road.

In Tomsk (not to be confused with Omsk)—the second-largest city in Siberia, and the only one with a university—the Flyer did catch up with the Protos. But not for long. The Germans had already been there a whole day, resting and making repairs, and were ready to leave. By the time the Americans got themselves and the car in shape to go on, the Protos was far ahead again.

Schuster insisted on making another all-night drive, with Miller relieving him. Since the roads were unusually good, they stepped up the pace, averaging as much as forty-five miles an hour. In the morning, MacAdam wrote, "we sighted the flying Protos less than two miles ahead. A most exciting race ensued. . . . Finally the American machine poked its nose right up against the German's gasoline tank, and Koeppen drew to one side to give it the road. As the Thomas flew by a great shout burst involuntarily from the throats of the four men on the car in unison. The Germans responded with the best of feeling, waving their hats and cheering." For the first time in three thousand miles, the Flyer was out in front. Though Schuster recalled that "Koeppen gave us a salute worthy of an ancient Teutonic knight," the lieutenant was not as cavalier about losing the lead as he seemed. He was, in fact, quite distressed. Like Schuster, he didn't care what the race committee said; the real winner, in his mind, would be the first car to reach Paris.

Later that same day, his distress turned to despair when the rear axle and differential, which had been giving them problems for some time, failed completely. While his mechanics did their best to repair the car, Koeppen took a train to the city of Ekaterinburg—which, during the Russian Revolution of 1917, would become notorious as the site where Tsar Nicholas II and his family were executed—to fetch the extra parts he had shipped ahead from Vladivostok.

He had a new axle sent to Omsk, which sat at the eastern edge of the vast plains of central Russia known as the steppes. Even before the Trans-Siberian Railway reached it, Omsk had been a prosperous city; thanks to its location on

LEFT: *The cars attracted crowds throughout their journey. Here a group of nomads surrounds the Thomas Flyer.*

BELOW: *Locals often chipped in to tow the cars out of trouble. Here the Thomas gets pulled out of a ditch.*

the Om River, it was the main shipping point for the grain and other crops that flourished on the fertile steppes.

The German mechanics managed to get the Protos as far as Omsk and install the axle before they themselves broke down. Both had fallen ill with malaria, contracted from the mosquitoes that had plagued them for much of the trip. They dosed themselves with quinine, but it was nearly a week before they were ready to travel again.

"And all the while," the lieutenant wrote, "the Thomas car increases its lead, and we have less room left to catch up. Our chances of winning seem to be almost zero. Only sheer luck and unrelenting willpower will help us in our fight for victory." If he had known what sort of luck lay ahead for the Flyer, he might have been less pessimistic.

Schuster had reached Omsk three days earlier, expecting the new transmission he needed so badly to be waiting for him. It wasn't, and no one could tell him where it might be. Assuming that the Protos was close behind them, the Americans had pressed on, hoping the "temporary" repairs they had made a month earlier would hold out a little longer. On the steppes thirty miles west of Omsk, MacAdam reported, they "encountered a swamp a mile wide. . . . The road had been covered with straw to prevent wagons from sinking, and the ferrymen warned the autoists of the depth of the swamp beneath, but Shuster [*sic*] refused to be stopped by any obstacle."

In trying to gun the car through the mud, he snapped two teeth off the driving gear. Men, women, and children from the nearest village had gathered to gape at the marvelous machine, the first auto ever to pass through the area; instead, they found themselves dragging the Flyer out of the swamp and into town. It must have been a bit of a letdown. Schuster returned to Omsk by *telega*, the traditional Russian horse-drawn vehicle, and sent off a series of telegrams in a fruitless effort to find the missing transmission. "I was in despair," he wrote. Then "a message came from Miller saying he had repaired the pinion. He had made some new teeth by driving in ordinary screws and filing them down. They worked!"

When the Flyer reached Ekaterinburg on July 6, Lieutenant Koeppen—who had taken the train there to order his new axle—was still there, waiting impatiently for his crew in Omsk to get back on their feet. Though he put up a brave front for the Americans' benefit, they sensed his frustration. "If the Protos arrives in Paris a week after you," he told Schuster, "it will be no disgrace considering what we have gone through."

Sending Captain Hansen ahead by rail to search for the lost transmission, the three Georges set out again, wondering how far Miller's jury-rigged driving gear would take them. From Ekaterinburg, the road climbed into the Ural Mountains, so gradually that the Thomas team barely noticed. At the highest point was a stone monument marking the boundary between Asia and Europe. The Americans paused long enough to scratch their names into the pillar.

George Miller scratches his name on the pillar signifying the dividing line between Europe and Asia.

Two continents down, one to go. Sixteen thousand miles traveled, five thousand to go.

The Zust, of course, was a lot farther than that from the finish line. Back when the Americans and the Germans were having one of their brief encounters in Tomsk, the Italians were just arriving in Chita, fifteen hundred miles to the east. But they were eating up the miles—as many as two hundred on a good day—and were confident of closing the gap.

Then, Scarfoglio wrote, "owing to one of the stupid, ridiculous incidents which are the joy of the pedestrian but the curse of the automobilist, we are held up once more." The reservoir that fed oil to the cylinders had run dry. Haaga, the long-suffering mechanic, borrowed a horse and rode off in search of lubricant. He returned with the news that "in the neighbouring country there was no other oil except that for the Singer sewing machines. He had collected the whole of it—thirty small bottles. . . . It was at least sufficient to put life into our motor."

Unfortunately, when they reached the next village they found that the lack of oil had ruined one of the engine bearings. Haaga wasted no time; with a shrug, he set to work casting a new one. "From a lump of mud he makes a mould. . . . Then, in an old iron spoon, over a fire of newspapers and pieces of a broken door, he melts half a dozen leaden bullets and cuttings from the bottom of a zinc pail. I watch him, wonder-struck." The homemade bearing kept them going for the next five days, until they could replace it with a proper one.

In spite of this minor triumph, Scarfoglio was feeling depressed. "It is the anniversary of my birth," he wrote on July 2, "and I am alone. . . . It is cold and this country is strange to me." But he wasn't entirely friendless. "Haaga and I drink a bottle of beer at the restaurant. '*Alla salute sua!*' said Haaga, raising his glass, and he had tears in his eyes." Though the German's command of Italian was still limited, he knew enough to toast his companion's health.

Like the other teams, the Italians had trouble finding ferries that were in working order. There were always villagers willing to help, but they wanted to be paid—handsomely. When Prince Borghese, the winner of the Peking–Paris race, passed through the area, he had been so free with his money that the locals assumed all foreign motorists must be rich. They "had organized for our benefit a service of boats and rafts at the fixed price of thirty roubles." By comparison, the ferries, when they were working, charged one ruble. On the day the Thomas entered Europe, the Zust had gotten no farther than Irkutsk, two thousand miles to the east. "The way is long," Scarfoglio told the *Times*, "and the goal is still far off, but human energy has its limits. We will take a short rest here."

JULY 9–JULY 22

When the results of the French Grand Prix, which had taken place on July 7, reached the crew of the Flyer, they felt even more pressure to make sure the American car was the first to reach Paris. The Grand Prix had been won by a German entry, a Mercedes that averaged sixty-nine miles per hour over the difficult course. Out of the next six runners-up, five were made in Germany. The Thomas car failed to finish the race.

Ironically, Monty Roberts, who had dropped out of the New York–Paris race in order to drive in the Grand Prix, never got the chance. He had been demoted to backup driver. When the Flyer reached Perm, the first large city west of the Urals, Schuster found a telegram from E. R. Thomas waiting for him: "DO YOU WANT US TO SEND MONTAGUE ROBERTS TO HELP YOU WHEN YOU GET ON THE GOOD ROADS OF EUROPE?" "This made me so mad," said Schuster, "I could have eaten nails. Was I to have only the bad roads? I took a drink of cognac and gave the operator . . . an answer saying nothing about Roberts but reporting I hoped to be in Paris about July 26."

His estimate, as it turned out, was a bit optimistic.

Beyond Perm, the roads were quite respectable; unfortunately, they were crowded with long caravans of wagons whose drivers had never encountered an automobile before. "They would shake their fists menacingly at us," wrote MacAdam, "and then, with a terrible scowl on their faces, would point to the open fields, indicating that we should take to the fields, and leave the road to the caravans."

The roar of the Flyer's engine, unabated by a muffler, startled the horses. One woman's team went so wild that "the wagon turned over, and the woman fell under it. She was slightly injured and almost frightened out of her wits. We picked her up and said something nice in English to her, after which we gave her $5 and hustled away."

Schuster, unwilling to entrust the ailing Flyer to anyone else, had gone back to doing most of the driving. He was getting most of the media attention, too. Ironically, after being in the shadow of Roberts for so long, he found himself on the receiving end of resentment. "Miller, usually a placid fellow, complained, 'You are getting all the credit.'"

They finally located the wayward transmission; it was in Kazan, 350 miles ahead of them. Recent rains had turned the roads to mud again, making driving difficult. Since they were so far ahead of the Protos, the other two Georges tried to convince their leader to give the Flyer and himself a rest. Schuster refused. "As long as the wheels will turn," he said, "I'm going to drive this car."

On the third day out of Perm, as they were climbing a steep hill, the team heard the cracking sound they had been dreading. The two temporary teeth had broken off the driving gear. The Flyer managed to creep along another fifteen miles before five more teeth snapped.

There was nothing to be done but to fetch the new transmission from Kazan. Schuster offered to let Miller go, pointing out that it was his chance to get some media attention for a change, but the mechanic declined. The journey to and from Kazan, by horse-drawn telega, used up four precious days.

"As I was drinking tea in a peasant hut on the return trip," Schuster wrote, "I heard the exhaust of a car. 'Automobile! Automobile!' shouted a woman. It was the Protos now ahead. I was too tired to go out and wave and it did not stop."

By the time the new transmission was installed in the Flyer, the Protos had a thirty-hour lead. The Americans continued to have problems, including a broken frame and a leaky radiator, but their worst experience wasn't the result of mechanical trouble. Though most of the rural Russians they encountered had been kind and helpful, on a stretch of road outside Vladimir the Americans met with outright hostility. Some of the locals shouted curses at them; some pelted them with sticks and stones; others had strewn broken glass on the ground and covered it with straw in an attempt to puncture the auto's tires. The team didn't learn until later the reason for the angry display: During the Peking–Paris race, an escort car sent out from Moscow to guide Prince Borghese had struck and killed a child in the area.

Lieutenant Koeppen's luck, which had lately been so bad, seemed to have turned. His crewmen had recovered from the malaria. The weather was decent, for a change. The roads were in good shape. So was the Protos. Aside from yet another broken leaf spring—the seventeenth since leaving Vladivostok—it had suffered no serious setbacks since leaving Omsk. When Koeppen piloted the car into Moscow on July 18, he was leading the Americans by thirty hours.

The city—which Scarfoglio would later describe as "a wave of white houses, surmounted by the gilded domes of the churches and the dark mass of the Kremlin"—was a major milestone for the Germans. From there on, they would have the same sort of "home field" advantage the Thomas team had enjoyed in America. Since there were Protos dealers throughout Europe—including one in Moscow—assistance and fuel and spare parts were never far away. Koeppen wasted no time in availing himself of the Protos Company's help. When the Moscow representative provided him with an escort, he lightened his own load by putting all his excess baggage aboard the other car.

The dealer also installed new springs on Koeppen's Protos. Despite these measures, the auto managed to break its suspension one more time before it got to St. Petersburg. Even with the delay caused by the broken spring, plus a couple of hours they reluctantly took off in order to catch some sleep, the crew covered the five hundred miles from Moscow to St. Petersburg in thirty-two hours.

St. Petersburg—the seat of Russia's ruler, Tsar Nicholas II, and a major cultural and industrial center—gave the Germans a warm welcome. As the first team to reach the capital city, they received the Imperial Automobile Club's thousand-dollar prize. In addition, a representative of the tsar presented them with a special medal.

From St. Petersburg, the race route headed southwest, along the shores of the Baltic Sea, through present-day Estonia, Latvia, and Lithuania. Before World War I redrew the map of Europe, Germany was much larger, stretching eastward along the Baltic through what is now northern Poland. As soon as the Protos crossed the Russian border, it was on German soil. The *Times* reported that the crew were "enthusiastically greeted by their fellow-countrymen, especially a number of the Lieutenant's brother officers" who gave him "the first assurances of the pride the Kaiser's army feels."

"Since the phenomenal showing of the German cars in the Grand Prix race at Dieppe," the paper noted, "there is a remarkable interest in the progress of the country's representative in the New York to Paris race. If a victory can be scored in this event, it will be held to clinch Germany's claim to the motor supremacy of the world."

For the past several days, no one had been quite sure where the Flyer was or how it was faring. Now Koeppen learned the whereabouts of the Americans, and it boosted his confidence considerably. "The Thomas is fully 400 miles and 36 hours behind us," he said. "I expect to . . . maintain our lead till we land in Paris definite winners."

He made no mention of the Zust. The Italian team, though, still considered themselves a part of the race. The problems they encountered after leaving Irkutsk on July 10 were mostly minor. They paid exorbitant fares to ferry operators; they slept in *zimskaya quarteras*, or hostels, where the beds consisted of planks suspended from the ceiling and the bedclothes swarmed with lice; they found nothing they could bear to eat except the usual bread, tea, and eggs; they drove through torrential rains and dense clouds of mosquitoes "as big as flies . . . whirling around us with a deafening buzz, which sometimes conquers the hum of the motor."

But overall, Scarfoglio wrote, "this terrible Siberia, from which we expected hostility and cruel reprisals, has turned out quite easy. . . . If we think of the terrible days in Buffalo and Michigan City, or of the mud in Iowa, it seems to us that Siberia is a paradise." Unfortunately, they would soon have reason to change their minds; Siberia would come to feel more like perdition.

JULY 23–JULY 30

The Protos's progress through Germany was nothing like the rest of the trip. It was not a road race; it was a triumphal tour. The car made terrible time because, in every village it passed through, it was mobbed by people waving German flags and cheering.

Thirty miles east of Berlin a convoy of fifty cars from the German Imperial Automobile Club met the team and escorted them into the city, where hundreds of thousands of fans were waiting to welcome the returning heroes. Among the revelers was Koeppen's white-haired father, a retired colonel, who was so proud that he broke down in tears.

As usual, the lieutenant got the lion's share of the attention. But when he was asked to give a speech, Koeppen showed that he had learned something more during the trip than just how to handle an automobile. He had learned humility. "I don't deserve credit for the car's good showing," he said. "The great dash across Russia, you see, was due entirely to the devotion and skill of my drivers, Caspar Neuberger and Robert Fuchs."

The Protos makes its way through Berlin, to the ecstatic cheers of the residents, proud to see the German car out front.

He also reminded the press that the race wasn't over yet. "Fortune has a habit of spoiling the best laid plans of mice and motor-cars. A reckless curve, an unfaithful tyre, any one of the thousand woes which lurk in ambush, may put us hopelessly out of the running." There was always the chance, too, that the Thomas would overtake them. Koeppen pretended to relish the prospect. "That would ensure a 'scorching' finish," he said, "and thus fill our cup of happiness to overflowing."

In reality, losing the lead to the Americans was his worst nightmare, and it seemed in danger of coming true. Soon after he arrived in Berlin, word reached him that, while the Protos was being held up by adoring crowds, the Thomas team was pulling another all-nighter and had just crossed the border into Germany.

Luckily, that proved to be only a rumor—"probably being inspired," said the *Times*, "by the nervous agitation of an overwrought populace, which feared the German car would be beaten into Paris."

But on the road out of Berlin, the Germans got another shock to their systems. When they asked a bridge-tender for directions to the next village, the man informed them that a car with the words "New York–Paris" on the side had passed through a half hour earlier. "We look at each other in consternation," wrote Koeppen. "There it is! Our nervousness was not without reason. But how was this possible? 'Damnation!' says Neuberger. 'Could it really be the Americans?'"

They put on as much speed as they could and before long spotted an auto throwing up a dust cloud ahead—it was the car the bridge-tender had told them about. But it wasn't the Thomas Flyer. It was one of the vehicles that had escorted them into Berlin, now on its way home. Stuck in its radiator were two flags that read, "New York to Paris."

Germany and France, who considered themselves the leaders of the automotive industry, also took great pride in their well-engineered and well-maintained highway systems. After 163 days of struggling over the world's worst roads, or no roads at all, for the next two days, Koeppen and his crew had the luxury of driving on some of the world's best. And after six months of blown tires and broken springs, the Protos experienced no problems at all during the final dash from Berlin to Paris. On July 26, Koeppen and his men entered the French capital. "We've reached our destination!" exulted the lieutenant. "We have completed our drive around the world, and are the first to finish."

But compared to the hero's welcome they had received in Berlin, their reception was disappointing to say the least. At 6:15 P.M. the Germans pulled up in front of *Le Matin*'s offices. "In the vestibule, we find a group of men assembled; the editor of the newspaper gives a speech congratulating us on behalf of all the members of the committee. . . . After a short while, we drive to our hotel."

The *Times* reported that "for some reason, possibly not unconnected with national feelings which time has not quite assuaged, there was no official ceremony or reception." Once the De Dion dropped out, the French had largely lost interest in the race; *Le Matin*'s coverage had dwindled to an occasional paragraph on the back page of the paper.

As far as Koeppen was concerned, he had won. He had fulfilled his duty to kaiser and country—and had done it with five days to go on his six-month leave. In the flush of victory, he seemed to have forgotten all the problems that had plagued him and his companions throughout the journey. "We have had a splendid trip," he told reporters, "and I'd like to take another such."

Even if he truly meant it, there was no way he could have afforded it. The expenses he'd incurred during the race came to some twenty-five thousand dollars. Koeppen was personally responsible for most of that. To make matters worse, when Knape and Maas withdrew, he had promised to reimburse them for the money they'd invested. The bottom line was, he was ten thousand dollars in debt.

And really, as the *Times* reminded its readers, "In spite of the Protos's leading the way into Paris, it is not the winner of the race." Technically, in order to finish in first place, all the Thomas had to do was reach Paris sometime in the next thirty days.

But Schuster admitted, "With everything happening, I was not sure of getting to Paris within a month of the Protos." Hansen, the team's only Russian speaker, had left the car temporarily to visit his wife in Moscow. As a result, MacAdam reported, "The car had wasted much time on the road by losing its way, through inability of the crew to make the Russians understand the sign language."

Then there were the inevitable mechanical problems, including a broken motor support, a leaky radiator, and a broken headlight, incurred when the car ran into a flock of pigeons. When the Americans reached Moscow, Hansen rejoined them. They were laid up there for two days, making repairs, and didn't reach St. Petersburg until July 22, the day the Protos entered Germany.

Schuster was determined to catch up at any cost. "We drove throughout the night and the next day," he wrote, "fighting sleep and fatigue. Miller relieved me at driving but he was equally weary, and I awoke once and grabbed the wheel just in time to keep the Thomas from going into a ditch." On July 27 the Americans reached Berlin. "Lieutenant Koeppen's father . . . and others greeted us and said the Protos had arrived in Paris the night before. They seemed unmindful of the penalty against Koeppen . . . and thought he had won. I did not argue."

Schuster expected to make the run from Berlin to Paris in two days or less. But, wrote MacAdam, "Dame Fortune seems to have conspired to delay the arrival of the American Thomas car in Paris." First they were beset by dense fog, then the clutch shaft gave out, and "for sixteen hours Schuster and Miller worked under a wayside appletree repairing the break."

Finally, on the evening of July 30, the Flyer entered the outskirts of Paris, only to be delayed yet again—not by Dame Fortune, but by an officer of the law, who meant to arrest them for driving with a broken headlight. "A man on a bicycle came forward," wrote MacAdam, "and offered his lantern to the crew, but it could not be detached from the machine. Finally the bicycle was lifted boldly on to the front seat of the automobile . . . and the car was allowed to proceed."

Aside from that gendarme, the people of Paris welcomed the Thomas team with far more enthusiasm than they had shown the Germans. According to the *Times*, "All agreed in declaring the performance the most remarkable ever undertaken in the history of sport and hailed the crew as heroes." Though Commissioner General St. Chaffray was still smarting from his own failure to finish the race, he dutifully threw a party in their honor.

"Schuster is much broken nervously by the hard trip," MacAdam observed, "but is the happiest man in Paris to-night, nevertheless." In addition to being exhausted, Schuster was unaccustomed to being the center of attention, and the speech he made to the celebrants was not nearly as glib or as gracious as Koeppen's had been. In fact, at times it was downright grim. "It has been a wonderful journey," he said, "and I cannot help but be pleased with the results. On the other hand, it has been extremely hard. We have constantly lacked sleep, and often have had nothing to eat. If it had not been for the fresh air we inhaled all the time, probably none of us would have been able to stand the hardships. Siberia is certainly no place for the automobile, but it's all over now."

Back in Buffalo, E. R. Thomas was giving the press a far more glowing assessment of the race, one that focused less on the crew than on the car. "That the Thomas, a simple stock car, should not only finish, but should be the only car to cover the official route and win by twenty-six days, defeating all the specially built foreign machines, proves that America is years ahead in the building of service cars. . . . The Thomas is reported to be in excellent condition, and . . . could start from Paris to-day and come back over the same route."

That was, to say the least, a wild exaggeration. Unless it were totally rebuilt from the wheels up, the only way the Flyer could possibly make it back to New York was aboard a ship. And even if E. R. Thomas had ordered the car overhauled, he would have had to find someone else to drive it. "We are glad to have made the trip," said Schuster, "but none of the three of us would undertake it again for anything in the world."

If asked, the crew of the Zust would surely have echoed those sentiments. While the Germans were being cheered in Berlin, Scarfoglio and Haaga were in Omsk, laboring over their auto. When the Protos left Germany, the Italian team *still* hadn't left Omsk. When Schuster was making his speech in Paris, the Italian team was still making repairs in Omsk. "Our poor machine," wrote Scarfoglio, "has been wounded and harassed by these six months of continual fatigue and travel on broken and impracticable roads. . . . It is patched and pieced and full of bandages and scars, like an old warrior."

JULY 31–AUGUST 14

Though both the German and American teams were claiming victory, the decision was ultimately up to the members of the race committee. They took their time about it. Before the Thomas even got to Paris, the German press and the Imperial German Automobile Club had begun lobbying to have their country's team declared the winner. They argued, as Koeppen had, that the rules had originally called for the cars to be shipped by train across part of the United States, so Koeppen shouldn't have been penalized for doing just that.

Once the Americans had arrived in Paris, the *Times* pointed out that, even if the fifteen-day penalty were removed, the Americans still had a fifteen-day handicap because of the trip to Alaska, and they had finished only four days behind the Protos.

Though Schuster hadn't cared to argue the point while he was on Koeppen's turf, he later expressed his feelings on the matter: "When I was younger and used to ride a bicycle in the road races, we would find some foxy fellow who would start in the race, ride a short distance outside of the city and after all the racers had started would turn back and cross the finishing point first, claiming the race. It was just such a deal as that the Germans tried to work."

A week after the Flyer had arrived in Paris, the race committee finally announced its ruling: The Thomas was officially declared the winner, by twenty-six days. The three Georges, who had loaded themselves and their car aboard a steamer in Le Havre the day before the announcement, wouldn't be absolutely certain that they had won until they landed in New York ten days later.

As far as the German and American teams were concerned, the race was over. But it wouldn't really be over until the last contestants reached Paris— or until they gave up, whichever came first. After all they'd gone through, Scarfoglio and Haaga weren't about to pack it in now, with a mere five thousand miles to go.

After an entire week in Omsk—where the hotel charged a substantial fee for every service and amenity, from sheets and blankets to bathwater, even the electricity to light their room—they finally set off again, on August 2. That night they stayed in another of those dreadful zimskaya quarters.

During a conversation with a rather nosy fellow guest, they made a few mild complaints about Russian roads and the state of the country in general. Later, they woke to find their room full of soldiers and officials who accused them of being spies, employed by some of those Russian political exiles in Siberia. The Zust had been impounded and was being searched for incriminating evidence.

The situation looked serious until the racers produced a document provided by the Russian race committee, stating that they had the approval of the tsar himself. Then, Scarfoglio said, "they went away, one by one, embarrassed, smiling, obsequious . . . continuing to salute us respectfully."

On August 6, after a night in another zimskaya, Haaga couldn't manage to drag himself out of the heap of furs that served as a bed. He was "suffering from the most atrocious colic, and his spasms are fearful." Doses of laudanum and quinine from their medicine chest had little effect.

Scarfoglio sent for a doctor, only to discover that "as far as I can make out he knows as much of medicine as I do—perhaps a little less." The best the doctor could offer, in return for his fee of ten rubles, was that Haaga suffered from "an affectation of the chest; it may be that it is indigestion." Scarfoglio "seized the charlatan by the shoulders, turned him round and kicked him out." Haaga's fever grew worse, and he became delirious. His companion was frantic with worry. "Alone, ignorant, and in a strange country . . . I did not know what to do. I gave him such remedies as were in my power, and watched over him for three days and nights."

Finally, the fever broke and Haaga began to recover. By August 12, the mechanic was so impatient to get rolling again that, despite his weak condition, he insisted on tinkering with the car. Scarfoglio noted with relief that "he sang as he worked." They set out again the following day; a day later they were in Ekaterinburg. Next stop, Europe.

AUGUST 15–SEPTEMBER 17

On August 15, the steamship bearing the Flyer and its crew docked in New York. Though the car was far from being in "excellent condition," as E. R. Thomas had boasted, it was in good enough shape to lead a victory parade through the streets of the city. Schuster insisted that Monty Roberts ride along with him and Miller and get his fair share of the glory.

Five days later, the three men drove the Flyer to Sagamore Hill, the summer residence of President Theodore Roosevelt. Roosevelt, the first president to learn to drive—and the first to be stopped for speeding—wanted a look at the celebrated auto and its crew. "I admire Americans who do things," he told them, "whether it is going up in a balloon, or down in a submarine, or driving an automobile around the world."

Though the Zust team weren't Americans, Roosevelt would surely have admired them, too, and their utter determination to finish the race against all odds. They were so worn down, Scarfoglio wrote, that "we no longer feel the desire to see and to know. We pass through all this strange and unknown land with absent eyes and indifferent minds, like old men who have already seen too much."

The one sight they were eager to see was the boundary marker that would indicate they had entered Europe; it represented a major milestone for them. When they were well west of Ekaterinburg and still had seen no hint that they were leaving Asia, they asked a mounted policeman, "How many versts to the Urals?"

The man burst into laughter. "But you have passed them half an hour ago. You are in Europe now."

"We were bewildered," wrote Scarfoglio. "To cross a chain of mountains and not to perceive it seemed to be too much altogether."

It seemed at first that, in entering Europe, they had left their troubles behind. The sun came out, Scarfoglio claimed, for the first time since they left Irkutsk. After seven months of keeping their thoughts to themselves, "Haaga and I speak without ceasing of the most ridiculous and useless things, from the mere necessity of talking and hearing the sound of our own voices."

In Perm, where they took a day off to let Haaga rest, they met a transplanted Frenchwoman. Homesick for her native country, she asked the men to "kiss the first girl you see when you arrive on French soil. If she resists, tell her it is for the sake of a poor exile."

Just west of Nizhny Novgorod, they got their first indication that bad luck, their longtime companion, hadn't departed; it had only taken a brief vacation. On a muddy road, the car skidded out of control and flipped over, throwing them from the vehicle. The men weren't injured, but the front axle was badly bent. Unperturbed as always, Haaga removed it and hauled it to the nearest village to be straightened.

When they reached Moscow on August 23, they were greeted with such enthusiasm that they felt like "prodigal children returned after long years of absence." For the first time, they learned that the Protos and the Thomas had

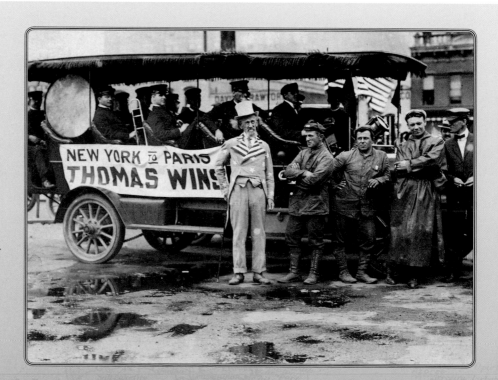

The Thomas Flyer receives a boisterous welcome on its return to New York City. Here "Uncle Sam" greets Schuster (second from left) and Miller (center), standing with their old teammate Monty Roberts (second from right).

arrived in Paris nearly a month before. The news made no difference to the Italian team. They had long ago abandoned any hope of winning; they wanted only to complete what they had begun. By August 26, they were on the road again. For several days they suffered no more than the usual setbacks. They became hopelessly mired in mud. The worn-out drive chains jumped off the sprockets; in one fourteen-hour period, Haaga repaired them thirty-one times. When they neared the border of Germany, they began to feel they were almost home. Fate chose that moment to deal the worst blow of all. As they passed a boy playing by the road, a horse-drawn cart approached from the other direction. Startled by the noise of the Zust's engine, the team bolted and ran down the child.

The cart driver, who either failed to notice or didn't want to be blamed, kept going. The Italians were devastated. "We pick up the little corpse, wrap it in a covering, and place it as gently as possible, as though unwilling to disturb its sleep, in the hinder part of the machine on a heap of furs, and then cover it to hide it from our eyes."

E. R. Thomas (in the white hat), owner of the Thomas Company, examines the victorious American car in the company of George Schuster (center). The original driver, Monty Roberts, is on the far right.

Since there was no sign of the boy's family, they drove to the nearest police station. The police had already learned of the tragedy via the telegraph, and, assuming that the foreign motorists were at fault, threw them in jail.

"It is all over now," wrote Scarfoglio, "and there is no escape. We have fought against all the difficulties and triumphed over everything. . . . But how shall we find strength to fight against and overcome the Russian police. It is all over now!"

They shared their cell with "fourteen delinquents who spoke all the languages of the world—except our own, naturally. . . . For three days we lived in a corner of that room seated on a hard bench, eating a few spoonfuls of the daily bean soup, scarcely daring to sip a drop of the infected water from a jug, and not speaking a word."

To their immense relief, the police finally uncovered the truth and released them. "Once more," Scarfoglio exulted, "we have conquered and escaped from the snares set for us by the cruel destiny which pursues us."

On September 6, the Italian team entered Berlin and were welcomed by "a fury of festivities." Scarfoglio observed that "the good Germans regard us in a certain sense as the moral victors in the race, through which we have travelled more loyally than all the rest, perspiring for mile after mile, and measuring the ground inch by inch."

But "cruel destiny" wasn't finished with them yet. The excellent German roads lulled Haaga into complacency; one afternoon, after eating and drinking a bit too heavily at an inn, he nodded off and ran the car into an embankment. When he came to, he and Scarfoglio were lying in hospital beds, bruised and bandaged. The Zust was in even worse shape; one wheel was smashed, the springs were broken, and the axle was bent again.

It was nearly a week before the car and its crew were able to go on. "This last blow of destiny," wrote Scarfoglio, "has only increased our determination to finish the course. An easy journey along this magnificent road would have been too mean an ending to our race. We shall have to struggle against fate until the last day."

When they crossed the border into France, Scarfoglio remembered his promise to the sad exile they had met back in Perm. He explained his mission to the first Frenchwoman they met, and she gladly let him kiss her.

On September 17, they entered Paris at last and were greeted by "speeches, champagne, toasts, congratulations." To his surprise, Scarfoglio felt no great sense of accomplishment. He felt, he said, no differently than he had eight months before, when he sailed from France to begin the race. "It is the same, and we are the same as then . . . as though the adventure were beginning today . . . And to think that we have traversed the world yard by yard to come here to gather happiness, that we have made this the ardent dream of all our nights, the goal of all our efforts! . . . But it is the destiny of man that all beautiful things wither in his grasp."

THE AFTERMATH

One reason Scarfoglio found so little joy in finishing the race was that he considered himself and Haaga the rightful winners. In his opinion, Koeppen should have been disqualified for shipping the Protos part of the way by rail. And he still insisted that, without all the preferential treatment the Thomas team had gotten back in America—having ready access to parts, being towed repeatedly, given permission to use the railroad tracks when the Zust wasn't—they would never have reached San Francisco first.

What he—or any of the contestants or automakers—neglected to mention was that, without teams of horses to tow them, and railroad tracks to drive on when the roads were hopeless, *none* of the cars would have made it across the United States, or Asia, for that matter.

The Automobile Club of America wasted no time in declaring the race "the most convincing demonstration of the ability of the modern automobile that could be afforded." But what the contest really demonstrated was that the automobile's ability was *limited*. No standard car, however well built or durable, could be expected to plow through ten-foot snowdrifts or knee-deep mud.

Automobiles would not be accepted by the general public as a reliable, everyday means of transportation, like the horse and the train, until there was a network of well-maintained all-weather roads for them to travel on.

Europe had already made a lot of progress in that direction, and the race made it clear that America had a lot of catching up to do. As one auto manufacturer observed, "The American who buys an automobile finds himself with this great difficulty: he has nowhere to use it."

Within five years, the situation would begin to change. The day the contestants set out from New York, the *Times* had predicted that "over their route the world's traffic will move some day." And, in the United States at least, that prediction proved accurate. By 1913, plans were under way to build the country's first transcontinental road, the Lincoln Highway. For most of its length, it followed the same route as the racers. In 1916, the Federal Road Act provided government funds for a system of interstate highways.

Though the race painted a poor picture of American roads, it put the country's automobile industry in an excellent light. "The American manufacturers," reported the *Times*, "are naturally delighted with the successes attending the Thomas, arguing that it shows that the American car can compete on an equal footing with the foreign-made machine." Between 1908 and 1909, sales of American-made autos nearly doubled. By 1910 the United States was producing more cars than all other countries *combined*.

The Flyer's victory may have helped spur this sudden success. But the most important factor was another significant event that took place a few months after the race ended: the appearance of the Model T Ford.

Up to that point, most manufacturers had built their autos one at a time, tailoring them to the buyer's needs or tastes—an expensive process. Henry Ford took a different approach. "The way to make automobiles," he said, "is to make one automobile like another automobile, to make them all alike . . . just like one pin is like another pin when it comes from a pin factory."

His goal was to produce cars that were simple, easy to repair, and within the budget of an ordinary person. Instead of building each car to order, the

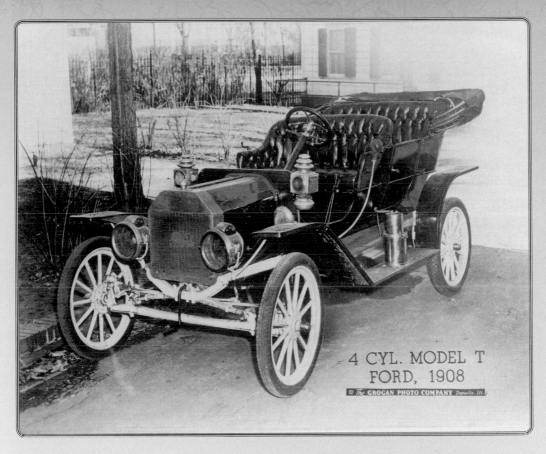

4 CYL. MODEL T
FORD, 1908

© *The* GROGAN PHOTO COMPANY *Danville, Ill.*

The 1908 Model T Ford, built on an assembly line, was a much more affordable car than the custom-made Thomas Flyer.

Ford Motor Company stuck to one standard model and made it as quickly and cheaply as possible, using a method pioneered by Oldsmobile several years earlier—the assembly line. As a result, the Model T sold for 850 dollars. In a time when five dollars a day was considered a good wage, that was still a lot of money, but pretty reasonable compared to the Flyer's four-thousand-dollar price tag.

Of course, the Model T wouldn't have sold well at any price if it hadn't been reliable. In June 1909, Henry Ford tested his car's mettle the same way E. R. Thomas had tested the Flyer—by entering it in a long-distance race. This one began in New York, too, but ended in Seattle. The famous Flyer, which E. R. Thomas was touting as the "champion endurance car of the world," took part, not as an official entry, but as a sort of advance scout. George Miller was at the wheel.

Like the unfortunate Auguste Pons, Henry Ford believed that smaller was better. His car weighed only twelve hundred pounds, and had a twenty-horsepower engine. The smallest of its competitors weighed more than twice as much, and had more than double the horsepower.

Unlike Pons's Sizaire-Naudin, the Model T won handily, crossing the country in twenty-two days. The Flyer never reached Seattle. It broke down in Idaho, just as the Protos had, and was shipped back to the factory by train.

Henry Ford's simple, affordable car went on to become a phenomenon. By 1916, the company was selling over half a million Model Ts each year.

The Thomas, like many other high-priced autos, just couldn't compete. The company enjoyed a temporary boost in sales as a result of the New York–Paris race, but its success didn't last long. Unfortunately, the new models weren't as well designed or as well built as the 1907 machine that won the race. According to Schuster, "The model L, the first shaft-driven Thomas, was noisy, underpowered, and literally leaked oil. . . . Several hundred cars came back to the factory, and many of the best Thomas dealers . . . quit selling Flyers and turned to other makes." The company's reputation quickly went downhill, and it 1913 it was declared bankrupt.

George Schuster remained loyal to the company until the bitter end. When he returned home from Paris, there were rumors that E. R. Thomas planned to give him a ten-thousand-dollar bonus for winning the race. To Schuster's disappointment it was no more than a rumor. "This thing has cost nearly $100,000," Thomas told him, "and we just don't have that kind of money." Schuster did receive the thousand-dollar bonus he'd been promised. He earned another 650 dollars by writing—or at least attaching his name to—overblown testimonials singing the praises of the wheels, the headlights, the springs, and other accessories used on the Flyer.

For a brief time, he toured New York and New Jersey with a member of the Automobile Club of America, presenting a lantern-slide lecture on the race. If Schuster had gone on touring with the show, he might have made a good income, but he was no public speaker, and he'd had his fill of traveling. He used the bonus money to make a down payment on a house and returned to his job at the Thomas factory.

When the quality of the cars began to decline, Schuster warned his boss about it, but was accused of being too much of a perfectionist. "Things became so unpleasant," he wrote, "that when Charles Henshaw, the Thomas distributor in Boston, wanted me to be his service manager, I took the job." After the Thomas Company went under, Schuster became a Ford dealer for a time, then switched to selling Dodges.

E. R. Thomas had offered to give him the Flyer he had driven to Paris, but the car was in such poor shape after its ordeal that Schuster turned it down. When the company's assets were auctioned off, the "Famous New York to Paris Racer" went to a Buffalo newspaper publisher, who left it sitting in his yard, rusting away. In 1948, the owner of the Long Island Auto Museum bought the car for his collection. Schuster was invited to visit the museum and be photographed with the car, but he wasn't convinced it was really the original vehicle.

In the early 1960s, Nevada gambling tycoon and automobile collector William F. Harrah purchased the car and flew its former driver, then ninety-one years old, to Reno to make a positive identification. Whatever doubts Schuster still had were dispelled when Harrah's mechanics took apart the clutch and he saw the holes he had drilled in the flywheel fifty-six years earlier, while making repairs in Moscow. His reunion with the car must have stirred old memories; a year later he wrote *The Longest Auto Race*, based on notes he kept during the trip.

The fact that a Protos had circled the globe—and, in the opinion of most Germans, had won the race—didn't help the car's sales much. Like the Flyer, the Protos was just too pricey for most buyers. Not long after the race, the company was bought out by the Siemens Corporation, which continued to manufacture a

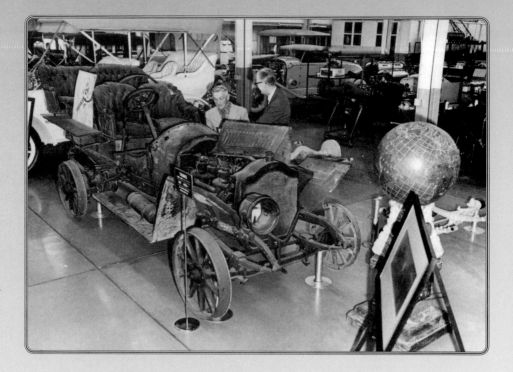

An elderly George Schuster examines the Thomas Flyer in the Harrah Museum in Reno, Nevada.

few autos until 1926. The car that made the long journey was enshrined in the Deutsches Museum in Munich.

Though Hans Koeppen was promoted to captain, he knew his army salary wasn't going to get him out of debt. As soon as he returned to Berlin, he set to work writing his account of the race. Published in November 1908 under the title *Im Auto um die Welt* (Around the World in an Auto), it was a best seller in Germany and put Koeppen in the black again. In the opinion of a *Times* reviewer, the book was "singularly free from boastfulness, straightforward and simple, and its criticisms are such as to leave no justifcation for bitterness in the minds of those criticised." Naturally, Koeppen did his best to convince the reader that his car was the true winner.

Only six years after the great race, the same sort of nationalistic sentiment that had inspired Koeppen and the other contestants—and made them dislike and distrust one another—led the countries of Europe into the Great War (World War I). Koeppen got his chance to fight in a bona fide battle at last. Unlike many of Germany's junior officers, he survived.

After retiring from active duty, he felt compelled to present his case to the world in a *second* memoir of the race, *Abenteuerliche Weltfahrt* (Round-the-World Adventure).

During World War II, the army called him up again and promoted him to the rank of general. Disillusioned by Hitler's policies, Koeppen soon resigned, pleading illness.

But that brief period of service cast a shadow over the rest of his life. After the war, he was nearly beaten to death by a group of Polish men when they learned that he had been a high-ranking officer for the Nazis. Then, despite his poor health, he was held prisoner by the Russians, who finally released him in 1947. He died a few months later.

The Zust Company went on turning out cars until the eve of World War I. Fortunately, not everyone who bought them suffered the same awful luck as Scarfoglio. Even when the race was over, cruel destiny continued to play tricks on him.

After recuperating in Paris, he took his auto on a publicity tour of England. As a mechanic was emptying the Zust's gas tank so the car could be put aboard a train, an acetylene lamp set the fuel on fire. The mechanic died in the blaze, and the rear half of the Zust was nearly destroyed. The manufacturer managed to restore it well enough to display it at an auto show in Paris.

No one seems to know for certain what became of it after that, but a British Columbia man who restores antique autos is convinced that a Zust he acquired thirty years ago is the same one that competed in the race. According to his records, the car made its way first to New York, then to Dawson City in Canada's Yukon Territory, where it was used as a taxi, then to Vancouver, where the present owner discovered it. The vehicle shows evidence of being repaired numerous times in the past, and many of the repairs match the ones that Haaga made to the original Zust.

After the race, Scarfoglio continued to work as a reporter for *Il Mattino*, covering such historic events as the Turkish government's massacre of Armenians during World War I. He also founded Italy's first serious film magazine, *L'arte muta*. And he somehow found time to pen a long, rambling, opinionated but very engaging account of the great race, *Il giro del mondo in automobile*, published in the United States in 1909 as *Round the World in a Motor-Car*. When Benito Mussolini came to power in 1925, Scarfoglio resigned from *Il Mattino*, knowing he'd never be permitted to write anything critical of the fascist dictator or his repressive regime. He died in 1969.

In Paris, Captain Hansen had received an anonymous letter calling him a traitor because he had deserted the De Dion "for the filthy money of the Americans." Soon afterward, the captain disappeared. "He had a considerable amount of money," said MacAdam, the reporter, "and was to start for his home in Tomsk . . . but the latest advices . . . are that he has not shown up there and none of his friends have heard from him."

Hansen's hasty departure may have had something to do with the threatening letter. Or he may have been trying to avoid paying the ten thousand rubles he owed after losing his wager. The Norwegian government asked for the Thomas

The American edition of Antonio Scarfoglio's colorful race account

Company's help in locating the captain. Finally, in 1911, they learned what had become of him. There was nothing very mysterious or dramatic about it. He had simply moved from place to place, ending up in St. Petersburg, where—perhaps inspired by his race with Monty Roberts back in Omaha—he was operating a roller-skating rink.

As the American bicentennial approached, a group of auto enthusiasts began making plans for a 1976 race that would duplicate the entire route of the 1908 contest—except that the cars would be flown rather than shipped across the Pacific Ocean. But it was the Cold War era; the Soviet Union and the United States regarded each other as enemies. The Russian government, undoubtedly fearing there would be spies among the contestants, concluded that the idea was "just not practical."

When relations between the countries improved, so did the chances of successfully staging a race that included Russia. In 2008, Rally Partners, Inc., which sponsors a yearly cross-country vintage auto rally called the Great Race, organized a combination rally and race that began in New York City on May 30—a hundred years after the start of the original race—and ended in Paris. (In a rally, the goal is not to cross the finish line first, but to navigate a prescribed course in a given amount of time, no more and no less.)

At the time this was written, the list of likely entries included four very familiar names: Protos, Thomas Flyer, Zust, and De Dion—not the original autos, of course, but full-size, faithful replicas of them, built especially for a two-hour television documentary. *The Greatest Auto Race on Earth*, produced by Frame 30 Productions of Edmonton, Alberta, Canada, combines period photos of the cars and drivers, commentaries by automotive historians (including George Schuster's great-grandson), and dramatizations of events from the race, filmed on location using actors and the re-created cars.

Two types of entries competed in the Great Race 2008. The Schuster Class included autos that were at least twenty-five years old. The Innovation Class featured cars that use relatively new methods—alternative fuels or super-efficient engines, for example—to boost mileage and lower emissions.

According to the CEO of Rally Partners, the purpose of the race was to "test and prove automotive propulsion technologies that will transport the world's citizens in the twenty-first century."

Back in 1908, auto companies were mainly interested in proving that their vehicles could compete with the horse and the train. Today, with the world's oil reserves dwindling and auto emissions contributing to global warming, the stakes are much higher. The challenge facing today's automakers is not to produce cars that can travel around the world, but cars that use a minimum of energy and emit as little pollution as possible, and the great race they're involved in now is a race against time.

To learn more about the race

www.thegreatestautorace.com
Web site of the documentary *The Greatest Auto Race on Earth.*

www.greatrace.com/newsite/index.php/2008-new-york-to-paris
Details about the 2008 re-creation of the race.

www.thegreatautorace.com
A variety of material about the original race, including videos, events, and links to other sites.

BIBLIOGRAPHY

"Automobile Race From New York to Paris, The." *Current Literature*, April 1908, pp. 359–361.

Ahlgren, Carol, and David Anthone. "Bad Roads and Big Hearts: Nebraska and the Great Race of 1908." *Nebraska History* 73, no. 1 (Spring 1992): pp. 13–17.

"Alternative-Fuel Vehicles to Race Around the World in 2008." http://www.prnewswire.co.uk/cgi/news/release?id=164210

Andrews, Allen. *The Mad Motorists: The Great Peking–Paris Race of '07.* Philadelphia: Lippincott, 1965.

"Antonio Scarfolgio & the Great Race of 1908." http://faculty.ed.umuc.edu/~jmatthew/naples/greatrace.htm

Buffalo Courier, September 8, 1908.

Chesterton Tribune, February 20, February 27, 1908.

Cole, Dermot. *Hard Driving: The 1908 Auto Race from New York to Paris.* New York: Paragon House, 1991.

Crabb, Richard. *Birth of a Giant: The Men and Incidents That Gave America the Motorcar.* Philadelphia: Chilton, 1969.

Clymer, Floyd. *Those Wonderful Old Automobiles.* New York: Bonanza, 1953.

Duncan, Dayton. *Horatio's Drive: America's First Road Trip.* New York: Knopf, 2003.

E. R. Thomas Motor Company. *The Story of the New York to Paris Race.* 1908. Reprinted as *New York to Paris, 1908*, Los Angeles: Floyd Clymer, 1951.

Fenster, Julie M. *Race of the Century: The Heroic True Story of the 1908 New York to Paris Auto Race.* New York: Crown, 2005.

Georgano, Nick. *The American Automobile: A Centenary, 1893–1993.* New York: Smithmark, 1992.

Koeppen, Hans. *Abenteuerliche Weltfahrt: Deutscher Sieg im Ersten Auto Rennen Um die Welt.* Braunschweig: Georg Westermann, 1935.

Lay, M. G. *Ways of the World: A History of the World's Roads and of the Vehicles That Used Them.* New Brunswick, NJ: Rutgers University Press, 1992.

Mahl, Jeff. "Was It the Men or the Machine?" *The Horseless Carriage Gazette*, January/February 1994.

New York Times, January 4–November 22, 1908; June 17, 1984.

Nicholson, T. R. *Adventurer's Road: The Story of Pekin–Paris, 1907 and New York–Paris, 1908.* New York: Rinehart, 1957.

Rae, John B. *The American Automobile. A Brief History.* Chicago: University of Chicago Press, 1965.

Scarfoglio, Antonio. *Round the World in a Motor-Car.* Translated by J. Parker Heyes. New York: Mitchell Kennerley, 1909.

Schuster, George, with Tom Mahoney. *The Longest Auto Race.* New York: John Day, 1966.

Scott, Jack B. *The Big Race: The Story of the First Transcontinental Race from New York to Seattle, 1909.* Raytown, MO: Jack B. Scott, *n.d.*

Sears, Stephen W. *The American Heritage History of the Automobile in America.* New York: American Heritage, 1977.

Ware, Michael E. *Making of the Motor Car: 1895–1930.* Hartington, Derbyshire: Moorland, 1976.

Whiticar, Alise Barton. *The Long Road: The Story of the Race Around the World by Automobile in 1908.* Ft. Lauderdale, FL: Wake-Brook House, 1971.

"World 35,000 km New York to Paris 2008 Racer's Guide." http://www.greatrace.com/pdfs/Racer_Guide_2008.pdf

NOTES

INTRODUCTION
Page 15: "The night was melancholy": *New York Times*, June 5, 1908.

THE PLAN
Page 17: "The supreme use" and "Is there anyone": Andrews, *The Mad Motorists*, p. 14.
Page 17: "a real Jules Verne undertaking": Andrews, *The Mad Motorists*, p. 15.
Page 17: "All competitors finishing": Nicholson, *Adventurer's Road*, p. 9.
Page 21: "As long as a man": Andrews, *The Mad Motorists*, p. 5.
Page 22: "impractical and foolhardy": *New York Times*, January 16, 1908.
Page 22: "A preliminary survey": Cole, *Hard Driving*, p. 14.
Page 22: "Busy trying to make" and "exceeding the upper": *New York Times*, February 11, 1908.
Page 23: "It must be borne": Schuster, *The Longest Auto Race*, p. 17.
Page 23: "an ingenious toy": Ware, *Making of the Motor Car*, p. i.
Page 23: "the motor-car": Andrews, *The Mad Motorists*, p. 65.

THE CARS
Page 24: "that automobile which": *New York Times*, January 5, 1908.
Page 25: "the most remarkable": *New York Times*, February 2, 1908.
Page 25: "Because of its size": Koeppen, *Abenteuerliche Weltfahrt*, p. 26.
Page 26: "solid as a battering ram": Whiticar, *The Long Road*, p. 42.
Page 26: "the best prepared" and "many of the devices": *New York Times*, February 2, 1908.
Page 28: "There you can see": Koeppen, *Abenteuerliche Weltfahrt*, pp. 28–29.
Page 30: "None of those": Schuster, *The Longest Auto Race*, p. 12.
Page 30: "It would be a disgrace": *New York Times*, February 17, 1908.
Page 30: "confident not only": *New York Times*, February 9, 1908.
Page 30: "We do not consider" and "advertising purposes": *Chesterton Tribune*, February 27, 1908.

Page 32: "It will be": *New York Times*, February 2, 1908.

THE MEN
Page 37: "the famous command": *New York Times*, July 25, 1908.
Page 38: "an amateur driver": *New York Times*, February 9, 1908.
Page 38: "this big, blond baby": Scarfoglio, *Round the World in a Motor-Car*, p. 47.
Page 39: "a better man": *New York Times*, February 9, 1908.

THE RACE, FEBRUARY 11–17
Page 40: "be in Paris": Whiticar, *The Long Road*, p. 62.
Page 42: "Patriotism has made": *New York Times*, February 13, 1908.
Page 42: "I'll back an American": *New York Times*, January 26, 1908.
Page 43: "the terrible German race": Scarfoglio, *Round the World in a Motor-Car*, p. 218.
Page 43: "Each nation seems": Scarfoglio, *Round the World in a Motor-Car*, p. 27.
Page 43: "between two thick" and "kissed again": Scarfoglio, *Round the World in a Motor-Car*, p. 28
Page 43: "Italy! Italy!": Scarfoglio, *Round the World in a Motor-Car*, p. 26.
Page 43: "Farness is better": Fenster, *Race of the Century*, p. 181.
Page 45: "Who goes slowly": Cole, *Hard Driving*, p. 45.
Page 45: "this soft yet": Scarfoglio, *Round the World in a Motor-Car*, p. 36.
Page 46: "We shovel snow" and "But we have": "The Automobile Race From New York to Paris." *Current Literature*, April, 1908, p. 359.
Page 46: "A slip of the wheel": Cole, *Hard Driving*, p. 47.
Page 46: "The chains wrapped": Scarfoglio, *Round the World in a Motor-Car*, p. 39.
Page 47: "My heart is full" and "We're here for the night": *New York Times*, February 16, 1908.
Page 47: "as if understanding": Scarfoglio, *Round the World in a Motor-Car*, p. 43.
Page 48: "We will await" and "The race": Schuster, *The Longest Auto Race*, p. 32.

Page 48: "Thank God": Koeppen, *Abenteuerliche Weltfahrt*, p. 41.

Page 48: "What terrible roads": Fenster, *Race of the Century*, p. 87.

Page 49: "a most unfortunate racer": *New York Times*, February 19, 1908.

FEBRUARY 18–MARCH 3

Page 50: "One of the features": *New York Times*, February 19, 1908.

Page 50: "much worse than": *New York Times*, February 21, 1908.

Page 50: "fragments of glass" and "a gigantic sword": Scarfoglio, *Round the World in a Motor-Car*, p. 53.

Page 50: "It gives the Thomas": *New York Times*, February 22, 1908.

Page 50: "The difficulty of automobile": *Chesterton Tribune*, February 20, 1908.

Pages 51–52: "candidly confess": Scarfoglio, *Round the World in a Motor-Car*, pp. 60–61.

Page 52: "I am the nephew,": Cole, *Hard Driving*, p. 52.

Page 52: "mistook the gallant,": *New York Times*, February 27, 1908.

Page 52: "I shall enter": *New York Times*, February 23, 1908.

Page 52: "One of the most": *New York Times*, February 16, 1908.

Page 53: "The American town": Scarfoglio, *Round the World in a Motor-Car*, p. 41.

Page 53: "Chicago lives by": Scarfoglio, *Round the World in a Motor-Car*, p. 71.

Page 54: "The whole truth": *New York Times*, March 1, 1908.

Page 54: "He loved to pose": Fenster, *Race of the Century*, p. 108.

Page 54: "Either you step": Koeppen, *Abenteuerliche Weltfahrt*, p. 57.

Page 54: "I had to laugh": Koeppen, *Abenteuerliche Weltfahrt*, p. 60.

Page 55: "Indeed, with our": *New York Times*, February 27, 1908.

Page 55: "They charge them": *New York Times*, March 2, 1908.

Page 55: "ALL CARS MUST DRIVE": Schuster, *The Longest Auto Race*, p. 49.

MARCH 4–20

Page 56: "the grandest reception": *New York Times*, March 5, 1908.

Page 57: "the most wide-awake": Cole, *Hard Driving*, p. 90.

Page 59: "one common sentiment": Scarfoglio, *Round the World in a Motor-Car*, pp. 87–88.

Page 59: "a body of ladies": Scarfoglio, *Round the World in a Motor-Car*, p. 81.

Page 59: "Civilization and brandy": Scarfoglio, *Round the World in a Motor-Car*, p. 78.

Page 59: "It is impossible": Scarfoglio, *Round the World in a Motor-Car*, p. 82.

Page 60: "In the twinkle": Scarfoglio, *Round the World in a Motor-Car*, p. 94.

Page 60: "the companion of our pilgrimage": Scarfoglio, *Round the World in a Motor-Car*, p. 92.

Page 60: "Then, mad with terror": Scarfoglio, *Round the World in a Motor-Car*, p. 109.

Pages 60–61: "the most exciting . . . into the timber": *New York Times*, March 21, 1908.

Page 61: "The most ferocious": Scarfoglio, *Round the World in a Motor-Car*, p. 148.

Page 61: "When the leaders": *New York Times*, March 8, 1908.

Page 62: "The succession of misfortunes": *New York Times*, March 10.

Page 62: "I cannot continue": *New York Times*, March 19, 1908.

Page 62: "I will win yet": Cole, *Hard Driving*, p. 115.

MARCH 21–APRIL 7

Page 63: "a splendid driver": Schuster, *The Longest Auto Race*, p. 73.

Pages 63–64: "It had taken": Schuster, *The Longest Auto Race*, p. 71.

Page 64: "the attempt to cross": *New York Times*, March 28, 1908.

Page 64: "the capital of the West": *New York Times*, April 8, 1908.

Page 64: "Wear this": Schuster, *The Longest Auto Race*, p. 73.

Page 66: "It seemed an": Schuster, *The Longest Auto Race*, p. 77.

Page 67: "a peculiar, inexplicable sound": Scarfoglio, *Round the World in a Motor-Car*, p. 120.

Page 67: "a fine fat" and "some patriotic Yankee": Scarfoglio, *Round the World in a Motor-Car*, p. 121.

Page 67: "Sitori had a moment": Scarfoglio, *Round the World in a Motor-Car*, p. 125.

Page 68: "greeted us with": Scarfoglio, *Round the World in a Motor-Car*, p. 137.

Page 68: "The town has": Scarfoglio, *Round the World in a Motor-Car*, p. 139.

Page 68: "like shipwrecked mariners": Scarfoglio, *Round the World in a Motor-Car*, p. 140.

Page 68: "We seem to be" and "singing horrible": *New York Times*, April 7, 1908.

Page 69: "furiously, as a wild" and "After fifty days": *New York Times*, April 8, 1908.

Page 69: "in a race": *New York Times*, April 7, 1908.

Page 69: "The De Dion car": *New York Times*, March 22, 1908.

Page 69: "It seems to me" and "No matter how good": *New York Times*, March 24, 1908.

Page 69: "He took out": *New York Times*, March 28, 1908.

Page 70: "Just what we expected" and "As a sign": *New York Times*, April 8, 1908.

Page 71: "It is no race": Fenster, *Race of the Century*, p. 225.

Page 71: "This race across": Cole, *Hard Driving*, p. 115.

Page 72: "Bad roads": Cole, *Hard Driving*, p. 117.

APRIL 8–APRIL 21

Page 72: "Because of submarine": *New York Times*, April 9, 1908.

Page 72: "Ours was the first" and "the impossibility": Schuster, *The Longest Auto Race*, p. 77.

Page 72: "a raven flashed": *New York Times*, April 11, 1908.

Page 72: "RETURN TO SEATTLE": Schuster, *The Longest Auto Race*, p. 81.

Pages 72–74: "Thus ends the daring": Scarfoglio, *Round the World in a Motor-Car*, pp. 156–157.

Page 75: "In its present": Fenster, *Race of the Century*, p. 232.

Page 76: "had telegraphed": Schuster, *The Longest Auto Race*, p. 82.

APRIL 22–MAY 16

Page 76: "The reward will come": Cole, *Hard Driving*, p. 54.

Page 77: "No serious difficulty": *New York Times*, May 17, 1908.

Page 77: "the machine broke": Cole, *Hard Driving*, p. 42.

Page 78: "the three brave": *New York Times*, May 18, 1908.

Page 78: "beautiful at night" and "a vulgar, banal city": Scarfoglio, *Round the World in a Motor-Car*, p. 169.

Page 78: "the De Dion": *New York Times*, May 18, 1908.

Page 79: "our opponents had gained": *New York Times*, May 17, 1908.

Page 79: "there was some": *New York Times*, May 8, 1908.

Page 81: "as springy as" and "climbed into the car": *New York Times*, May 15, 1908.

Page 81: "drunk with their": *New York Times*, May 17, 1908.

Page 81: "to cross the": Schuster, *The Longest Auto Race*, p. 91.

MAY 17–JUNE 5

Page 82: "In parts the road": *New York Times*, May 17, 1908.

Page 82: "dens of filth": Fenster, *Race of the Century*, p. 26.

Page 82: "Most disquieting rumors" and "They had heard": *New York Times*, May 29, 1908.

Page 83: "inspired by the keen": *New York Times*, May 20, 1908.

Page 83: "The car is in": *New York Times*, May 19, 1908.

Page 83: "As a German" and "arranged to provide": *New York Times*, May 20, 1908.

Page 83: "we never again": Fenster, *Race of the Century*, p. 257.

Page 84: "There is no petrol": Scarfoglio, *Round the World in a Motor-Car*, p. 216.

Page 84: "He further said": *New York Times*, May 21, 1908.

Page 85: "Vladivostock was intended": Scarfoglio, *Round the World in a Motor-Car*, p. 215.

Page 85: "I tucked the little": Schuster, *The Longest Auto Race*, p. 94.

Page 86: "was a streak": Schuster, *The Longest Auto Race*, p. 94.

Page 86: "so deep in the mud": Schuster, *The Longest Auto Race*, p. 95.

Page 86: "Lieutenant Koeppen": Schuster, *The Longest Auto Race*, p. 95.

Page 87: "The only place," "we heard a whistle," and "We were able": *New York Times*, May 29, 1908.

Page 87: "the country was infested": Schuster, *The Longest Auto Race*, p. 99.

Page 89: "Four miles inside": Schuster, *The Longest Auto Race*, p. 101.

Page 89: "The TIMES's correspondent," "two soldiers," and "became a scenic": *New York Times*, June 5, 1908.

Pages 90–91: "[Sitori] has been": Scarfoglio, *Round the World in a Motor-Car*, pp. 218–219.

Page 91: "We notice that": *New York Times*, June 2, 1908.

Page 91: "reached an arrangement": *New York Times*, June 7, 1908.

Page 91: "the wretched town": Scarfoglio, *Round the World in a Motor-Car*, p. 219.

JUNE 6–JUNE 25

Page 93: "without warning": Koeppen, *Abenteuerliche Weltfahrt*, p. 182.

Page 93: "pushed the car": *New York Times*, June 17, 1908.

Page 94: "You do that" and "If there is any": Cole, *Hard Driving*, p.172.

Page 94: "several threatening letters": *New York Times*, June 13, 1908.

Page 94: "At home we could": *New York Times*, August 16, 1908.

Page 95: "This car smells": Schuster, *The Longest Auto Race*, p. 104.

Page 96: "a complication": Scarfoglio, *Round the World in a Motor-Car*, p. 220.

Page 96: "The plain all round" and "We dismounted": Scarfoglio, *Round the World in a Motor-Car*, p. 225–226.

Page 96: "There is another": Scarfoglio, *Round the World in a Motor-Car*, p. 227.

Page 96: "this announcement afforded": Scarfoglio, *Round the World in a Motor-Car*, p. 239.

Page 96–97: "There are red-hot" and "feeling a little": Scarfoglio, *Round the World in a Motor-Car*, p. 240.

Page 97: "Haaga and I" and "a hundred paces": Scarfoglio, *Round the World in a Motor-Car*, p. 247.

Page 97: "two alleged Frankfort": Scarfoglio, *Round the World in a Motor-Car*, p. 248.

Page 97: "to feed eternally": Scarfoglio, *Round the World in a Motor-Car*, p. 303.

Page 98: "disasters, disasters": Scarfoglio, *Round the World in a Motor-Car*, p. 258.

JUNE 26–JULY 8

Pages 98–99: "troubled by the image": *New York Times*, July 27, 1908.

Page 99: "Half the people": *New York Times*, July 28, 1908.

Page 99: "We had decided" and "so that one": Schuster, *The Longest Auto Race*, p. 109.

Page 100: "we sighted the flying": *New York Times*, July 1, 1908.

Page 100: "Koeppen gave us": Schuster, *The Longest Auto Race*, p. 113.

Page 102: "And all the while": Koeppen, *Abenteuerliche Weltfahrt*, p. 210.

Page 102: "encountered a swamp": *New York Times*, July 5, 1908.

Page 102: "I was in despair": Schuster, *The Longest Auto Race*, p. 114.

Page 103: "If the Protos": Schuster, *The Longest Auto Race*, p. 119.

Page 104: "owing to one": Scarfoglio, *Round the World in a Motor-Car*, p. 265.

Page 104: "in the neighbouring" : Scarfoglio, *Round the World in a Motor-Car*, p. 266.

Page 104: "From a lump": Scarfoglio, *Round the World in a Motor-Car*, p. 267.

Page 104: "It is the anniversary" and "Haaga and I": Scarfoglio, *Round the World in a Motor-Car*, p. 269.

Page 105: "had organized": Scarfoglio, *Round the World in a Motor-Car*, p. 277.

Page 105: "The way is long": *New York Times*, July 10, 1908.

JULY 9–JULY 22

Page 105: "DO YOU WANT" and "This made me": Schuster, *The Longest Auto Race*, pp. 119–120.

Pages 105–106: "They would shake" and "the wagon turned": *New York Times*, August 16, 1908.

Page 106: "Miller, usually" and "As long as": Schuster, *The Longest Auto Race*, p. 120.

Page 106: "As I was drinking": Schuster, *The Longest Auto Race*, p. 122.

Page 107: "a wave of": Scarfoglio, *Round the World in a Motor-Car*, p. 349.

Page 108: "enthusiastically greeted": *New York Times*, July 23, 1908.

Page 108: "Since the phenomenal": *New York Times*, July 19, 1908.

Page 108: "The Thomas is": *New York Times*, July 23, 1908.

Page 108: "as big as flies" and "this terrible Siberia": Scarfoglio, *Round the World in a Motor-Car*, pp. 299–300.

JULY 23–JULY 30

Page 109: "I don't deserve": Fenster, *Race of the Century*, p. 332.

Page 110: "Fortune has a habit" and "That would ensure": Whiticar, *The Long Road*, pp. 328–329.

Page 110: "probably being inspired": *New York Times*, July 25, 1908.

Page 110: "We look at each other": Koeppen, *Abenteuerliche Weltfahrt*, p. 263.

Page 111: "We've reached our" and "In the vestibule": Koeppen, *Abenteuerliche Weltfahrt*, p. 266.

Page 111: "for some reason": *New York Times*, July 27, 1908.

Page 111: "We have had": *New York Times*, July 27, 1908.

Page 111: "In spite of": *New York Times*, July 27, 1908.

Page 111: "With everything happening": Schuster, *The Longest Auto Race*, p. 120.

Page 112: "The car had wasted": *New York Times*, July 23, 1908.

Page 112: "We drove throughout": Schuster, *The Longest Auto Race*, p. 126.

Page 112: "Lieutenant Koeppen's father": Schuster, *The Longest Auto Race*, p. 129.

Page 112: "Dame Fortune" and "for sixteen hours": *New York Times*, July 30, 1908.

Page 112: "A man on a bicycle": *New York Times*, July 31, 1908.

Page 112: "All agreed in declaring": *New York Times*, July 31, 1908.

Page 114: "Schuster is much" and "It has been": *New York Times*, July 31, 1908.

Page 114: "That the Thomas": *New York Times*, July 31, 1908.

Page 114: "We are glad": Schuster, *The Longest Auto Race*, p. 133.

Page 114: "Our poor machine": Scarfoglio, *Round the World in a Motor-Car*, p. 309.

July 31–August 14

Page 115: "When I was younger": *Buffalo Courier*, September 8, 1908.

Page 116: "they went away": Scarfoglio, *Round the World in a Motor-Car*, p. 317.

Page 116: "suffering from": Scarfoglio, *Round the World in a Motor-Car*, p. 318.

Page 116: "as far as I can," "an affectation," "seized the charlatan," and "Alone, ignorant": Scarfoglio, *Round the World in a Motor-Car*, pp. 319–321.

Page 116: "he sang": Scarfoglio, *Round the World in a Motor-Car*, p. 322.

August 15–September 17

Page 117: "I admire Americans": Schuster, *The Longest Auto Race*, p. 138.

Page 117: "we no longer feel": Scarfoglio, *Round the World in a Motor-Car*, pp. 333–334.

Page 117: "How many versts," "But you have passed," and "We were bewildered": Scarfoglio, *Round the World in a Motor-Car*, pp. 328–329.

Pages 117–118: "Haaga and I": Scarfoglio, *Round the World in a Motor-Car*, p. 331.

Page 118: "kiss the first": Scarfoglio, *Round the World in a Motor-Car*, pp. 334–335.

Page 118: "prodigal children": Scarfoglio, *Round the World in a Motor-Car*, p. 350.

Page 119: "We pick up": Scarfoglio, *Round the World in a Motor-Car*, p. 356.

Page 120: "It is all over": Scarfoglio, *Round the World in a Motor-Car*, p. 358.

Page 120: "fourteen delinquents": Scarfoglio, *Round the World in a Motor-Car*, p. 359.

Page 120: "Once more": Scarfoglio, *Round the World in a Motor-Car*, p. 359.

Page 120: "a fury of festivities" and "the good Germans": Scarfoglio, *Round the World in a Motor-Car*, pp. 361–362.

Page 120: "This last blow": Scarfoglio, *Round the World in a Motor-Car*, p. 363.

Page 121: "speeches, champagne" and "It is the same": Scarfoglio, *Round the World in a Motor-Car*, p. 368.

The Aftermath

Page 121: "the most convincing": *New York Times*, July 31, 1908.

Page 122: "The American who": Lay, *Ways of the World*, p. 159.

Page 122: "over their route": Whiticar, *The Long Road*, p. 67.

Page 122: "The American manufacturers": *New York Times*, July 31, 1908.

Page 122: "The way to make": Rae, *The American Automobile*, p. 59.

Page 124: "The model L": Schuster, *The Longest Auto Race*, pp. 143–144.

Page 124: "This thing has cost": Schuster, *The Longest Auto Race*, p. 140.

Page 125: "Things became so": Schuster, *The Longest Auto Race*, p. 144.

Page 126: "singularly free": *New York Times*, November 22, 1908.

Page 128: "for the filthy" and "He had a considerable": Cole, *Hard Driving*, p. 206.

Page 129: "just not practical": Cole, *Hard Driving*, p. 224.

Page 130: "test and prove": "Alternative-Fuel Vehicles to Race Around the World in 2008."

INDEX

PERM

VLADIMIR

ST. PETERSBURG

Baltic
Sea

Moscow ✪

NIZHNY
NOVGOROD

KAZAN

EKATERINBURG

BERLIN ✪

GERMAN EMPIRE

Paris ✪

EUROPE

FRANCE